The Privilege of Prayer

Laying the Foundation
for the
Work of the Church

Eugene A. Smith

The Privilege of Prayer

Word & Worship Global Outreach
www.wwgo.ca

ISBN: 1-931178-59-3

All scripture quotations are taken from
the New King James Version
(all bold face is added by the author)

Published by:

Vision Publishing
1520 Main Street – Suite C
Ramona, CA 92065
USA

www.vision.edu

This book is dedicated to all our friends who have prayed so passionately and earnestly for Darla, me, and our two sons.

You brought us through to victory during a deep trial.

This ministry has blossomed because of your faithfulness.

Table of Contents

Section Four:
Power by Prayer

Section Five:
Perseverance in Prayer

Section Six:
Pathway to Prayer

Section Seven:
Participating in Christ's Prayer

Section One

The Pattern of Prayer

Section One

Section One

The Pattern of Prayer (1)

God Looks for Intercessors

So God created man in His own image; in the image of God He created him; male and female He created them. Then God blessed them, and God said to them, "Be fruitful and multiply; fill the earth and subdue it; have dominion over the fish of the sea, over the birds of the air, and over every living thing that moves on the earth." (Gen. 1:27-28)

"And they heard the sound of the Lord God walking in the garden in the cool of the day," (Gen 3:8)

The first progenitors of the human race heard not only the sound of the Lord walking in the garden in the cool of the day, but also His call to them. When Adam responded, the first recorded conversation between God and man was initiated. It is reasonable to assume that the Creator often visited the Garden of Eden and enjoyed conversing with Adam and Eve, edifying and instructing them.

God is still calling out to mankind, inviting all to come into His presence. By the shed blood of Jesus, everyone is urged to enter into the holiest place, where God Himself dwells, and to draw near to Him (Heb. 10:19-22). We are encouraged to come boldly to the throne of grace, that we may obtain mercy and find grace to help in time of need (Heb. 4:16). The Word of God declares not only that God created mankind for His pleasure (Rev. 4:11), but also that the prayer of the upright is His delight (Pro. 15:8). Indeed, it boldly states that God, our heavenly Father, desires to provide our needs and to fulfill our lives (Lk. 11:11-13; Matt. 6:8). He expects us to be anxious for nothing, and to bring every detail of our lives to Him in prayer. (See Phil. 4:6-7.)

What a blessing! What an honor! Indeed, it is a privilege beyond description to be invited before the throne from which God rules the universe, and to bring to Him all our petitions. The Scripture encourages us to believe that our prayer moves the hand of God. Scripture boldly declares that the effective, fervent prayer of a righteous man avails much (James 5:16).

In addition to sharing our lives with the Lord, He has ordained that we work together with Him concerning His will. Through prayer, we are invited to join with Him in the accomplishment of His heart's desires. How is this possible? The Holy Spirit searches the deep things of God (1 Cor. 2:10). He not only reveals God's will to us but also creates it in us. Then, we utter God's will back to Him in prayer. By prayer, we participate with God in the performance of His will.

Common Misconceptions

Because many people are confused about such concepts as the sovereignty of God and the power of Satan, they have misconceptions about prayer, and they naturally project these into their communications with God. Some well-meaning but misguided saints always associate prayer with spiritual warfare. Inadvertently, they spend more time talking to the devil than they do talking to God. Unfortunately, a considerable portion of the teaching on prayer in Christian circles is nothing but human con-

The Privilege of Prayer

jecture that is not based on any sound interpretation or approach to the Scriptures.

Either consciously or unconsciously, we all approach the subject of prayer from a specific perspective. This viewpoint affects the content of our prayer and the manner in which we pray. Some spend far more time talking to "mountains" than they do petitioning God concerning situations for which they require His assistance. For some, it is quite common to address the Lord in one breath and to talk to the devil in the next. Others think of prayer as the means by which certain desired results are obtained. Still others appear to have no ability to pray without being preoccupied with some form of "spiritual warfare" because, to them, prayer is the means of "binding and loosing."

These views of the purpose of prayer fall short of the Biblical perspective. They seriously undermine a true understanding of the sovereignty of God, exaggerate the power of the forces of darkness, and fail to grasp the larger purposes of God. If God has permitted Satan to "sift" one like wheat as in the case of Peter (Lk. 22:31-32), someone "binding Satan" can accomplish nothing worthwhile. In such a case, the person would be opposing the will of God. Would it not be more correct to pray that the person's faith not fail? That is how Jesus prayed for Peter.

So often prayer is treated as if it is some sort of magical formula. Other people's lives and circumstances can be altered as we dictate orders! Prayer has become a means of manipulation as we give commands according to our own understanding, maturity, and point of view.

To some, prayer is the means of enforcing a "triumphalism." Triumphalism sees all of salvation in the past tense, and all that is needed is to enforce the victory that Christ has given at the cross. This view of prayer fails to see that salvation still has a future tense, and that the world is still in a fallen state and that God will use it to His advantage in dealing with the affairs of men. This cannot be the true scriptural representation of prayer.

If we believe that the power of the Holy Spirit is given to enforce Calvary's victory over the devil, most likely a series of commands spoken to the devil will consume our prayer time. Praise, no longer considered something offered to a worthy God, becomes the prime weapon in our spiritual battles. Then, prayer meetings are not times when the church corporately brings issues before God, but occasions for pulling down strongholds. Binding and loosing have replaced prayer and worship.

However, if we see that Satan is totally under the authority of God, and that he and his evil host work within the bounds of God's permission, prayer takes on a totally different role. As Jesus' parable regarding the widow suggests, we are to discuss with God the difficulties encountered because of the adversary (Lk. 18:3). Paul did not rebuke the devil concerning the thorn in his flesh; he took the matter to God in prayer (2 Cor. 12:7-8). After asking God three times to remove the thorn, Paul received the answer, "My grace is sufficient for you, for My strength is made perfect in weakness." (2 Cor. 12:9). Thus, in dealing with the subject of prayer, many inferences are made that assist our understanding of other subjects in Scripture.

A Definition of Prayer

Prayer is neither telling God what to do nor forcing our will upon others. It is not the manipulation to our liking of events or circumstances. **Prayer is agreeing with God concerning what He has revealed He desires to do.** Consequently, the Father's desires will be achieved on earth as they are in heaven (Matt. 6:10).

God requires His people to pray before He acts. This is abundantly clear throughout Scripture. The plagues upon Egypt were removed after the earnest and passionate pleas by Moses to the Lord (Ex. 8:12-13,30-31; 9:28-33). Nehemiah poured out his heart to God for Jerusalem (Neh. 1:4-11). Jeremiah was pained at his very heart (Jer. 4:19), and he wept many tears over Jerusalem (Lam. 3:48-49). Paul prayed without ceasing for the many churches he knew. (See 1 Thess. 3:10; Col. 1:3.)

It may seem a strange thing that God would have us pray before He acts and performs His will. The prophet Ezekiel gave a glowing list of things God would do to restore His people (Eze. 36:21-38). However, God does not want His people to assume that all this is automatic. Before He will perform His promises, He instructs them, "Thus says the Lord God: I will also let the house of Israel inquire of Me to do it for them;" (Eze. 36:37). God will not act until we pray.

This perhaps is one of the mysteries of prayer. Why does God require us to pray before He acts? Why has God designed His working so our prayer releases His power and ability? Prayer may be likened to a set of railway tracks. No matter how powerful the train engine is, it cannot go anywhere if the tracks have not been laid.

How we respond to these questions will determine our attitude toward prayer. It is plain that God seeks intercessors so that He may accomplish His will. In Isaiah's time, a general lethargy had taken over the people, and there was none who stirred himself up to call upon the Lord (Is. 64:7). There are to be watchmen who call upon the Lord until He answers (Is. 62:6-7). God is astonished when there is no one to help and no one to uphold (Is. 63:5). He looks for champions and is amazed when there is no man or intercessor (Is. 59:16). God's complaint is that no one would make up the hedge and stand in the gap to avert judgment (Eze. 22:30-31).

Since this is the proper premise for understanding prayer, then it is no wonder that prayer is to be the first and chief work of the church (1 Tim. 2:1). It should leave us little room for surprise at the thought that prayerlessness is sin (1 Sam. 12:23).

Thankfully, there are many examples in Scripture of men and women of God who did stand in the gap, who did intercede, who were champions. Abraham continued to intercede until Lot was delivered (Gen. 18:22-33; 19:29). Daniel bowed his knee three times a day (Dan. 6:10-11). Having the mind of God through the Scriptures of his day, Daniel set himself to implore God not to forget his promise (Dan. 9:2-3). In his distress, the Psalmist lifted up his voice in the evening, morning, and noon (Ps. 55:17).

When compassed about with adversaries, David gave himself to prayer (Ps. 109:4). If need be, he would fast until his knees became weak and his flesh was feeble (Ps. 109:24). The Psalmist also praised seven times a day because of the Lord's righteous judgments (Ps. 119:164).

Jesus understood the necessity of prayer. Robed in flesh, He lived His life upon this earth with the same limitations that you and I have. His life was devoted to faithfulness in prayer. Before attempting to answer some of the mysteries of prayer, let us take encouragement from the life of Jesus by studying His devotion to prayer.

The Privilege of Prayer

Thought Questions

1. God declares that the prayer of the upright is His delight (Pro. 15:8). Who are the upright people?

2. In James 5:6, two adjectives (effective and fervent) are used to describe prayer that avails much. Describe this kind of prayer.

3. Have you ever engaged in prayer like you have described? Through prayer, we can join with God in accomplishing His heart's desires. How is this made possible?

4. Always associating prayer with spiritual warfare is an incorrect use of prayer. Discuss this statement.

The Pattern of Prayer

The Pattern of Prayer (2)

The Prayer Life of Jesus

Without doubt, Jesus was a man of prayer. Throughout His life, He was in constant communion with His Father. It was His habitual manner of life and the reason for His success in whatever the Father led Him to do. Even in His ascension, He always lives to make intercession (Heb. 7:25).

Before examining the prayer habits of Christ, it is necessary to make some comments on His humanity. Jesus Christ is God. When the Word was made flesh (Jn. 1:14), the Son of God did not lose any of His deity. At the same time, He became human in the full sense of the word. In Christ, God and man have been joined together.

Scripture records that He was tempted in all points as we are, yet He was without sin (Heb. 4:15). The Son of God moved into the realm of human experience and faced life as any other individual. He assumed the same experience as the children of men, that of flesh and blood (Heb. 2:14). In every respect, He was made like unto His brethren (Heb. 2:17). Truly, His divinity positioned within human limitations, Jesus lived His earthly life from the human perspective. He had to develop in wisdom and stature like anyone else (Lk. 2:52). Jesus grew and became strong in spirit, being filled with wisdom (Lk. 2:40), because of His dedication to frequent prayer (Lk. 22:39).

Jesus had to ascertain the will of God for His life in the same manner that anyone else does. Nothing came to Him without effort. Only through prayer and diligent application of the Scriptures did He discover His Father's plan for Him. From His human perspective, even He Himself did not know when He would be returning (Mk. 13:32).

At some point in His youth, He comprehended Who He was. At the age of twelve, having already been trained to an impressive degree in the Scriptures, He knew that His life's purpose was to be about His Father's business (Lk. 2:49). Over the next eighteen years, He continued to prepare Himself until the will of God was confirmed to Him through the voice of John the Baptist. He then knew through this witness that His Father's business was to bring in the long awaited kingdom of heaven that John had been announcing. When Jesus consecrated Himself to that work, by submitting Himself to John's baptism, the Father spoke from heaven, bringing further confirmation and direction (Lk. 3:21-22).

When the Father spoke from heaven, He quoted two Old Testament scriptures. One, from Psalm 2, identified Jesus as the Son of God. This psalm speaks of the majesty and authority of the great King Who inherits the heathen as His portion. The Father also quoted from Isaiah 42:1, stating that He delights in His servant. Thus there came an understanding that the King is the same as the servant of the Lord. The kingdom of heaven will be established on the principles of servanthood and not by worldly means of domination and force (c.f. Matt. 20:25-28). Satan, in the wilderness, attempted to move Jesus from this manner of doing the Father's will (Matt. 4:1-11).

After being publicly called, Jesus was immediately led aside into the wilderness for a season of prayer. He needed to hear God on several issues. How would the kingdom be inaugurated? How would He obtain the attention of the masses? What message would He speak? From where would the finances come? These are some of the issues that would be worked out through prayer and trial.

Spiritual work can only be accomplished by persevering, believing prayer, waiting upon God, and through fellowship with Him. The believer's first responsibility is to minister unto God. Direction, guidance, strength and renewal come by waiting upon Him. Spiritual life is maintained by a consistent prayer life. This is the example led by Christ. It is also the pattern of the early church as it ministered to the Lord (Acts 13:1-2). The prophet Ezekiel emphasized the same truth as God sought the priests to minister unto Him (Eze. 44:15).

Jesus devoted Himself to discerning the Father's will through prayer and set Himself aside to hear the Father's voice, even if that meant forty days of fasting (Lk. 4:2-4). Through watching and prayer, Jesus overcame the temptations of ambition, presumption, carnality, and self-sufficiency. Repeatedly, Jesus said that He did not come to speak His own words, do His own will, or perform His own works. He only did and spoke as he saw His Father initiate. (See Jn. 5:17,19,23; 6:57; 8:26-29,38; 10:18, 14:10,24,31; 20:21.) In this manner, He became our pattern. (See Matt. 26:36-41).

Mark records that Jesus arose a great deal before day, went into a solitary place, and prayed (Mk. 1:35). The evening before, He had ministered to a multitude of people, healing the sick and casting out demons. Virtue had gone out from Him; physical and spiritual exhaustion resulted. Even so, while others slept, Jesus arose early to renew Himself by prayer and fellowship with the Father. After that particular early morning, Jesus received new direction concerning where to go next.

The Pattern of Prayer

After Jesus had fed the five thousand in the wilderness, both the multitude and the disciples failed to understand the significance of the miracle. No one caught the significance that Jesus was demonstrating how His own body would be broken for all to receive eternal life. Subsequent to sending both the disciples and the crowd away, He again renewed Himself through prayer (Mk. 6:45-46).

Though all the gospels show Jesus in prayer, perhaps the gospel of Luke, in which the humanity of Jesus is highly emphasized, demonstrates this more than the others. For instance, Luke records that Jesus was in a posture of prayer when baptized by John (Lk. 3:21-22). As a result of prayer, the gift of the Spirit and the necessary anointing for His ministry came upon Him.

From the multitudes that had gathered about Him, Jesus called a few to be especially close to Him, to be taught and trained in the work of God. Before making these momentous decisions, He went out into the mountain and continued the whole night in prayer (Lk. 6:12-16). Jesus would not initiate anything by His own will because He had come to do the will of His Father. Therefore, He took every decision to His Father in prayer and continued in prayer until direction was given. This was His continuous lifestyle. (Compare Jn. 8:26-29,38.)

Luke discloses the great revelation that Peter received - Jesus is the Christ of God. This understanding came as a result of the prayer life of Christ (Lk. 9:18-20). Jesus was praying when He asked His disciples about the public's view and the disciples' opinions concerning Him. It was through prayer that they were helped in this basic revelation of the person of Christ.

On various occasions, the disciples needed to have their faith strengthened. Peter told the Lord that He did not need to go to the cross. Unknowingly, Peter had been the mouthpiece of Satan (Matt. 16:21-23). A short time after this, Jesus took Peter, James, and John into a mountain to pray. At this point, the transfiguration occurred, bolstering the faith of these disciples. All this happened because Jesus went to prayer (Lk. 9:28-36).

The disciples had been observing the prayer life of Jesus. They asked Jesus to teach them how to pray. Jesus responded by giving them what has become known as "The Lord's Prayer." (See Lk. 11:1-13.)

The faithful prayers of Christ continually sustained the disciples. Peter did not know himself: he boasted of great courage and displayed a heroic attitude when in reality he would very quickly deny knowing Christ. The death of Christ would be a mammoth trial to Peter's soul. How would Peter survive this shaking of everything he had believed? What would keep his faith from failing? It was Jesus' prayer on behalf of Peter that brought the disciple through (Lk. 22:31-32).

In His own moment of intense trial, Jesus, once again, retreated to prayer. In the Garden of Gethsemane, facing the cross, Jesus suffered such great agony that His sweat was as if it were great drops of blood falling to the ground. He committed Himself to the Father's will, even if it meant death, and was strengthened by prayer (Lk. 22:39-44).

Though it is well known that Jesus sought to hear God three times on this occasion, Matthew's record shows the progression of the revelation of God's will in this matter. In His first prayer, Jesus said, "If it is possible, let this cup pass from Me; nevertheless, not as I will, but as You will." No answer from heaven was heard. In His second prayer, Jesus now said "If this cup cannot pass away from Me unless I drink it, Your will be done." Notice the progression that has been made in understanding the Father's will (Matt. 26:38-42). He had prayed a third time and received assurance from His Father concerning the divine will.

Being strengthened for what was to take place that very night, He said to His disciples, "Behold, the hour is at hand, and the Son of Man is being betrayed into the hands of sinners." (Matt. 26:45). The writer of Hebrews, referring to this same incident, states that Jesus was heard because He reverenced God (Heb 5:7). In this story, Luke definitely refers to Jesus' normal habit of seeking out quiet places to devote Himself to prayer (Lk. 22:39). According to the comment in Mark's gospel, Jesus often needed to go into desert places to be alone (Mk. 1:45).

John's gospel, however, gives the most details of Jesus' prayers. At the "Last supper" Jesus states that He will pray the Father for the gift of the Spirit to be given (Jn. 14:16). Thus, because of Jesus' prayer, the ministry of the Holy Spirit was provided.

Before handing Himself over to be tried and crucified, Jesus gave Himself to prayer. His "High Priestly Prayer" is recorded in John 17:1-26. There He offered much prayer for His disciples. He would be going back to the Father from whence He came, having completed the work He was given to do. Thus, Jesus prays for the success of the ministry of the disciples, that they would be encouraged, sanctified, and empowered.

Though Jesus is now risen from the dead, ascended on high, and is seated at the right hand of Majesty, He has not ceased to intercede. He ever lives to make intercession for those who come to God by Him, thus being able to save them to the uttermost (Heb. 7:25). He can act as King in power because He first functions as Priest in prayer. By following Christ's pattern, believers become a kingdom of priests (Ex. 19:6; Rev. 1:6).

The Privilege of Prayer

The illustration of Christ's prayer life demonstrates that spiritual work requires fellowship with God first. In so doing, guidance, direction, and enablement are received. God initiates all spiritual work and only by communication with Him can it be established. Accomplishing God's work is done through constant reliance upon Him in prayer. Thus, waiting upon God and ministering to Him is the church's primary responsibility. May the church cry out, as did first disciples, "Lord teach us to pray!" (Lk. 11:1).

The Pattern of Prayer

Thought Questions

1. How did Jesus discover His Father's plan for Him?

2. Comment on the following statement: Christ's divinity was positioned within human limitations.

3. When Jesus died on the cross of Calvary, did His prayer ministry cease?

4. Before His death, Jesus prayed that the gift of the Holy Spirit would be given to His followers. What evidence is there that the Father answered His prayer?

5. Describe in general terms the prayer habits of Jesus.

Section Two

The Purpose of Prayer

Section Two

The Purpose of Prayer (1)

The Eternal Purpose and Prayer

God has ordained that the church inherit glory along with Christ. This is the constant theme throughout the Book of Romans. An often-quoted scripture verse states that all have sinned and fall short of the glory of God (Rom. 3:23). However, those who have been redeemed by the blood of Jesus rejoice in the hope of God's glory (Rom. 5:2); for glorification is the eternal purpose for the people of God (Rom. 8:28-30).

In the eighth chapter of Romans, Paul reveals both the climax of God's eternal purpose and the role of prayer in the life of the Spirit-filled believer. These two themes are closely related. A quick review of the first eight chapters of the Book of Romans will enable the reader to see how the Holy Spirit relates to God's purpose and, especially, why the Holy Spirit is the Spirit of prayer.

The whole world is guilty before God, both Jews and Gentiles. This is the emphasis in the first part of the epistle (Rom. 1:1 – 5:11). As the answer to sins committed, Paul puts forth doctrines such as justification, sanctification, and redemption through the blood of the cross. Then he carries this discussion further, emphasizing deliverance from the very power of sin (Rom. 5:12 – 6:23). This is accomplished in the believer by the cross, being crucified and resurrected with Christ. In chapter seven, deliverance from the law and the strength of sin are expounded. The wonderful truth of the enabling power of the Holy Spirit is then put forth in chapter eight, in which Paul speaks of God's purpose and the life of prayer. The believer's spiritual condition is on par with Adam's before he disobeyed God in the Garden of Eden.

This last statement may confuse some people. Though Adam was created perfect in the sense that he had come from the hand of God, he was not in his "final" state. God wanted him to develop, mature, and grow. Through obedience, he would become all that God intended for him and thus enter into his destiny of being glorified with Christ.

All of creation has a "teleological" direction to it. Jesus is preparing all of creation to be filled with Himself, and is moving it toward this specific end. Most Christians have looked at the incarnation (Christ becoming flesh) through the eyes of redemption only. However, if sin had not occurred, Christ still would become incarnate to unify the creation with His own glory. This is to occur at His "appearing."

But sin did enter creation and its effects needed to be undone. Thus, the atonement was the "occasion" of the incarnation, but not the ultimate purpose of it. The much higher purpose of uniting creation with Himself demands the believer's attention and focus. Thus, Jesus came physically to initiate the process of salvation by His death upon the cross and His glorious resurrection from the tomb. Already, He is glorified in His humanity.

Those who exercise faith in Christ have initiated their salvation and are justified. Their salvation will be finalized when Christ physically returns, at which time they will be glorified with Him. Salvation carries with it both a "past tense" and a "future tense" ranging from the first coming of Christ to His return. Justification may be likened to an espousal or betrothal while glorification may simulate a wedding.

This was God's original plan for Adam. The world was created perfect, but not in a glorified state. Christ was to come to unite creation with Himself, glorifying it; it was made for Him (Heb. 2:10). Adam, like the rest of creation, was created perfect but not glorified. Adam was to eat of the tree of life, to be obedient to God, and thus, to develop in the knowledge of God to prepare himself for the ultimate goal of creation, even outside the context of sin.

The believer's justification places him in the position Adam would have been in if he had not sinned. Justification now relates the believer back to God's original purpose. Many have made the Spirit-filled life, as described in Romans eight, the goal of the Christian life; Paul, however, makes it the beginning. The goal is glorification with Christ, at which time all of creation will be set free from the curse of sin and enter into its glorified state as well.

Perhaps the following diagram will illustrate this truth:

The Father loves the Son ------------------------------The Appearing of Christ
Glorification of Creation

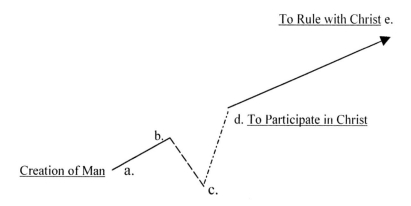

To Rule with Christ e.

d. To Participate in Christ

b.

Creation of Man a.

c.

Point (b) represents the fall of man. His movement towards the revealing of glory at the appearing of Christ was stopped. He fell short of the glory of God (Rom. 3:23). At point (c), man hears the call of the gospel of grace, receiving God's grace to cleanse him. He is restored to point (d). From here, man continues on, in God's originally designed purpose, to move towards point (e), the time of Christ's appearing. The appearing of Christ is not viewed as the end of salvation as much as it is understood as the climax of all eternity and the point to which all history is moving: the revelation of the glory of the Son of God in His inheritance from the Father in which man participates.

Point (d) is the point of justification. By justification, man now participates "in Christ' as originally designed by the Father. The ongoing ministry of the Holy Spirit in the believer continues from point (d) to point (e). This causes man to learn and share in Christ, again as the Father's original purpose states. At point (e), Christ appears in glory and man is raised from the dead. Salvation has concluded with glorification, which is the same as the Father's ultimate goal for His Son.

Thus, it should be seen that glorification with Christ has always been God's eternal goal for all of creation, especially for man who would receive the very life of the Son of God. Justification puts man back into the plan! This is the wonderful truth Paul is teaching in Romans 8:14-30:

> For as many as are led by the Spirit of God, these are the sons of God. For you did not receive the spirit of bondage again to fear, but you received the Spirit of adoption by whom we cry out, "Abba Father." The Spirit Himself bears witness with our spirit that we are children of God, and if children, then heirs – heirs of God and joint heirs

with Christ, if indeed we suffer with Him, that we may also be glorified together. For I consider that the sufferings of this present time are not worthy to be compared with the glory which shall be revealed in us. For the earnest expectation of the creation eagerly waits for the revealing of the sons of God. For the creation was subjected to futility, not willingly, but because of Him who subjected it in hope; because the creation itself also will be delivered from the bondage of corruption into the glorious liberty of the children of God. For we know that the whole creation groans and labors with birth pangs together until now. Not only that, but we also who have the firstfruits of the Spirit, even we ourselves groan within ourselves, eagerly waiting for the adoption, the redemption of our body. For we were saved in this hope, but hope that is seen is not hope; for why does one still hope for what he sees? But if we hope for what we do not see, we eagerly wait for it with perseverance. Likewise the Spirit also helps in our weaknesses. For we do not know what we should pray for as we ought, but the Spirit Himself makes intercession for us with groanings which cannot be uttered. Now He who searches the hearts knows what the mind of the Spirit is, because He makes intercession for the saints according to the will of God. And we know that all things work together for good to those who love God, to those who are the called according to His purpose. For whom He foreknew, He also predestined to be conformed to the image of His Son, that He might be the firstborn among many brethren. Moreover whom He predestined,

these He also called; whom He called, these He
also justified; and whom He justified, these He
also glorified.

In this passage, Paul makes a distinction between the children of
God and the sons of God who are yet to be manifested. In his
discussion, he also uses the word "adoption." The Biblical
meaning of adoption is much different from that of the western
world. The most common understanding would be to take an
orphaned child into your home and treat the child as your own,
even though he or she was not actually born to you. However,
this is not the practice to which Paul refers.

The Biblical meaning of adoption is more closely associated
with the idea of a graduation. Adoption changed the status of a
child to that of a son inheriting full rights. A father would place
his young child under tutors to be trained in the disciplines of
life, especially according to the interests and designs of the father. This training took place most often under a trusted slave,
who was inferior in status to the child being trained. When the
training was complete, the father adopted his own child who was
now placed in the status of a son, prepared and ready for work in
his father's interests. Adoption is simply the changing from a
child to a son.

Being born again, the believer is a child of God. Adoption occurs at the return of Christ, at which time his physical body is
redeemed (Rom. 8:23). At present, the believer has entered the
beginnings of salvation with the experience of justification.
Then, at that day, salvation is brought to its conclusion with glorification. Today, the believer is a child of God: then, he will be
adopted as a son of God. Thus, the believer is now being trained
and developed to participate in God's glorious eternal purpose
for His Son Who inherits all things. The believer will inherit

with Christ! This is the grand purpose of God: a design that includes participation by the believer as the Body of Christ in the Father's ultimate expression of eternal love for His Son. What a privilege!

What has all this to do with prayer? It has everything to do with it. Prayer is the foundation of the cry of the heart to God. In the day of glorification, the Holy Spirit will hold all of creation in perfect harmony and He will be the life and energy of the whole universe. Even the resurrected body will be a spiritual body - a body that is animated by the Spirit, in perfect harmony with God, executing to perfection the slightest whisper and desire of the inner man in the service of God.

The believer has received the firstfruits of the Spirit already. The gift of the Spirit in the interim before the adoption is called the "Spirit of adoption." The Spirit, Who is the agent of glorification, now prepares us for that glorification. Who are the sons of God who will be manifest on that day of adoption? They are those who are led by the Spirit and continually follow His leading, teaching, and guidance.

In that glorious day, the believer will know the "harvest" of the Spirit when He holds all in perfect harmony. Today, His guidance is the firstfruits of glorification. The Holy Spirit knows the purpose of God and works toward that final end. He bears witness within the believer. The Holy Spirit yearns for that day. His task is to prepare the Body of Christ for it. He yearns for the presence of sin to be removed from the face of creation and to bring it to its final state of participating in Christ's glorification. This is the Holy Spirit's burden and desire.

As the Spirit of adoption, the Holy Spirit teaches the church these things. His longings become the believer's as well. The saint is pulled toward the goal of God's purpose. He who knows freedom from the penalty of sin presently finds deliverance from its power through the Spirit, but also yearns for release from sin's very presence. The justified one longs to be glorified. He has tasted the powers of the age to come (Heb. 6:5). Knowing a good work has begun in him, he longs for it to be completed (Phil. 1:6). Just as the espoused person is anxious for the wedding date to arrive, so the believer cannot be satisfied with things as they are and is eager for his glorification. The student who has enrolled in a school is not content only with the learning process, but works toward completion, at which time he will be rewarded with graduation.

The Holy Spirit sees perfectly the plan of the Father for His Son. He yearns for the day that Christ will fill all things. These yearnings are felt within the spirit of the believer. The groanings of the Spirit become the hope of the believer and become the focus of his life. This hope causes a reformation of his will and desires. He now finds himself speaking of this, just as a bride-to-be gives constant attention to the upcoming wedding. These yearnings are the foundation of prayer.

As the believer comes into daily contact with this passing world, he feels a pull to better things. When he meets a situation that needs deliverance, the longing for a more noble reality naturally vents itself in prayer for the present circumstance to come into harmony with the future vision that fills his soul. Prayer is as natural as breathing to the one who is "saved" by hope, who has tasted things to come, and who has experienced the firstfruits of the Spirit.

Prayer is an essential part of life for the one whose mind, will, conscience, and emotions have been altered by the anticipation of glory. He constantly desires that the present would surrender to the future, the earnest to make way for the inheritance, the part to be complete in the whole, and for faith to give way to sight. From deep within his spirit, he cries out to God his Father that it be so.

The Spirit helps the believer in his deficiency. The believer does not know how to pray or for what to pray. However, the Holy Spirit does! He knows the mind of God perfectly and makes intercession accordingly. The intercessions of the Holy Spirit are felt within the longings in the spirit of the believer. The Holy Spirit calls out for God's will to be done. He continually intercedes for the needs of God's people, for the lost, to bring everything into reconciliation with God's will for creation's participation in the Son's glory. The Holy Spirit continually builds the church and longs to set the people free. He craves to deliver them from the captivity of sin and to bring all into the liberty of the Son of God. The Holy Spirit desires to possess the believer with great jealousy (James 4:5).

Intercession is the ministry of the Holy Spirit. He knows what to pray, when to pray, and how long to pray. His will and longings are felt in the believer's spirit. To be in intercession simply means to give voice in prayer to God of the travail within. He is given to the believer as the provision for all aspects of life, including prayer. From the Father, the Comforter has come to the believer, and now He leads the believer back to the presence of God (Jn. 15:26; Eph. 2:18).

Thus, a Spirit-filled life is the prerequisite for a dynamic prayer life. Those who are mastered by the Christian hope, the return of Christ to unite creation with Himself in glory, will be people of prayer. Though living in the present world, the believer knows and comprehends that his real and true citizenship is in heaven (Phil. 3:20). At present he is a stranger, sojourner and pilgrim (1

The Purpose of Prayer

Pet. 2:11). He has been persuaded of the promises and has been mastered by the sense of destiny as joint heirs with Christ (Heb. 11:13-14). He loves not this world (1 Jn. 2:15-17) for it has been judged at Calvary and is fading away (1 Cor. 7:31). Thus, the future hope of the believer has become the incentive for and the power in prayer.

It should be obvious that a life lived according to the flesh will never demonstrate a prayer life. A person who lives for the present age, for one's own pleasure, will not know the Holy Spirit's ushering into the presence of the Father. Those who live after the flesh are in danger of spiritual death (Rom. 8:12-13). By contrast, those who walk by the Spirit of God will suffer in this present world, but these sufferings are not worthy to be compared with the glory that shall be revealed (Rom. 8:17-18). Hallelujah!

The Privilege Of Prayer

Thought Questions

1. Determine the meaning of the following words: Justification, sanctification, redemption, and glorification. These words are frequently used in the text of this book. How do these concepts help you understand the salvation process?

2. "Many have made the Spirit-filled life, as described in Romans eight, the goal of the Christian life; Paul, however, makes it the beginning." Discuss this idea.

3. All creation is set free from its groanings and the sons of God are manifest. When will these things happen? Comment on the statement.

4. Explain how the believer's destiny of glory is the foundation for his prayer life.

The Purpose of Prayer

The Purpose of Prayer (2)

Why Should We Pray?

Many people have a variety of difficulties with the subject of prayer. Why pray at all? If God is all-powerful and nothing can stand in His way or oppose His will, then why does He not just do as He wishes? Why does He require us to pray before He acts? Why does He limit Himself to the prayer of the church? Does not His will then remain undone? Why is Satan permitted to exist and to try the saints? These questions reveal that there is some mystery to prayer; it is both simple and complex. They do not suggest that Christians should avoid warfare and opposition to the work of darkness. However, without a proper understanding of the purposes of prayer, these aspects become overbalanced and become a faulty basis of prayer, replacing the expression of the Holy Spirit's leading.

The answers to these questions are found in the eternal perspective, in seeing the purpose which God the Father has ordained for His Son. This has been discussed in the previous chapter, where we learned that God's goal for creation is for it to be united with Christ in a glorified state. The noblest part of creation is man, who was created to receive the very life of the Son of God. Thus, man would become a partaker of Christ and express the life of the Son of God. Many individuals corporately come together as the Body of Christ.

God the Father ordained before the beginning of time that all creation is for the sake of His Son, the heir of all things (Heb. 1:2; 2:10). By the incarnation, Christ would unite all creation with Himself and it would subsequently be filled with His glory at His appearing. The Father also ordained that His Son would receive a Body through which He would express Himself throughout the entire creation including the heavens and the earth. Since the fullness of the Godhead is in Christ (Col. 2:9), the Father and the Holy Spirit would also be given expression. The Father also ordained that Christ would be the head of this Body, as He is the head of all creation.

These things were ordained from before the foundation of the world. If sin had never occurred, these are still the goals of God. These goals will be fully achieved by God when Christ returns in His glory. All creation is set free from its groanings and the sons of God are manifest. This larger purpose of God is often lost in people's minds, being overshadowed by the wonderful story of redemption. Sin did occur and the coming of Christ must first undo the sad spiraling downfall of the human race. Thus, the first coming of Christ deals with the issue of sin, and His return will see the accomplishment of the eternal counsels of the Godhead.

Redemption simply allows man to qualify as a participant in the eternal purpose. Salvation is initiated with justification and will be brought to its completion at the return of Christ with glorification. A person who is born again is brought into a relationship with God, but is not yet at his final state. He is at the point Adam would have been if he had been obedient instead of choosing to disobey the command of God.

Redeemed man, joint-heir together with Him, is therefore in training for the full realization of his destiny as a member of the Body of Christ. As the passage of Romans 8:14-30 teaches, we are being developed for this glorious end by the Holy Spirit, otherwise known as the Spirit of adoption Who leads us in prayer. **Thus, it is revealed that prayer is the arena where our training and development takes place!** As joint-heirs with Christ through whom He expresses Himself and as His bride that shares His throne, we must be prepared for this role: it is not automatic. The lessons are to be learned now, in this life. So many people miss this simple perspective – life is a period of time in which we prepare for the ages to come.

It is imperative that we learn the art of effective authority and the humility for complete submission. We need to grasp the heart, burden, and desires of the Master. We must learn what pleases Him and brings Him glory. In order that we will be able to cooperate with Him in eternity, we must understand His aims and purposes. By allowing the Holy Spirit to teach us to pray, He will have opportunity to enlighten us in all matters of importance.

This is why God does not act until we pray. How can we rule and reign with Christ in eternity if we do not pray now? In meeting the conditions for prayer that moves the hand of God, we become qualified for participation in God's eternal purpose for His Son. Prayer is the school where the redeemed Body of Christ is tutored for its destiny. Successful prayer is dependent on a variety of conditions, all of which culminate and point to our ultimate end.

Impure motives are dealt with. Sin needs to be removed. Idolatry, stinginess, doubt, and unforgiveness are all being swept away by the Spirit Who teaches us to pray and to sympathize with the will of God. Our heavenly Teacher addresses even our lack of gratitude. To see the will of God carried out, we are being taught to abide in Christ and to stay in relationship with Him. The words of Christ must abide in us, having sway over us, so our will becomes harmonized with His. We are being taught the proper use of the name of Christ in prayer. This does not mean that invoking His name is some sort of means to get what we want, but the use of His name is for the sake of carrying out "business" for His sake, in His interest. Thus, the many lessons needed for qualification in the eternal purposes are learned in the school of prayer.

The Privilege Of Prayer

Thought Questions

1. Why does God not act until we pray? Consider this question carefully, and then write a response of no less than 300 words. Include in your discussion reference to God's eternal purpose.

The Purpose of Prayer

Section Three

Provision for Prayer

Section Three

Provision for Prayer (1)

The Holy Spirit and Prayer

Perhaps Samuel's comment frightens some believers. He stated that prayerlessness is sin (1 Sam. 12:23). Maybe some believers secretly feel that they cannot possibly obey Paul's admonition to "Pray without ceasing." (See 1 Thess. 5:17.) Yet the New Testament assumes that prayer is the primary function of the church and its most common activity (1 Tim. 2:1-2). Prayer was part of the foundational and continual experience of converts (Acts 2:41-42). It was the first duty of the apostles (Acts 6:4). Scripture also takes for granted that husbands and wives regularly pray together (1 Pet. 3:7).

In spite of all this, the most common weakness of both the individual believer and the corporate church seems to be a lack of prayer. Prayer meetings are generally the most poorly attended and are often relegated to a mid-week meeting. Why is this the case? Why do people not develop a strong prayer life? Often there is a secret feeling that a life of prayer is not possible; previous attempts at prayer have not produced fellowship with God. They have tried and have been disappointed. Perhaps it was too demanding on their time. Maybe it was a struggle because it seemed to be a very unnatural thing to do. Consequently, there was no strength to continue since the resolve was not strong enough. The call to repentance was heard, but there didn't seem to be the power to persevere in the place of prayer.

Paul recognized this deficiency and difficulty. All have this infirmity - we do not know how to pray or for what to pray (Rom.

Provision for Prayer

8:26). Here, just as He is in every other area of Christian living, the wonderful gift of the Spirit is the answer. It is the Spirit who gives life. The flesh profits nothing (Jn. 6:63). They that are in the flesh cannot please God (Rom. 8:8).

Perhaps, believers in their attempts to pray become more aware of their struggle with the flesh. What a revelation to see that intercession is the ministry of the Holy Spirit! Love, joy, and peace are the fruit of the Spirit and not the result of self-will. Prophesy, gifts of healing, and workings of miracles are gifts of the Spirit; they are not natural ability. Likewise, the Holy Spirit is the One Who makes effective prayer possible. Since we do not know how to pray for things as we ought, the Holy Spirit makes intercession for us.

> "Likewise the Spirit also helps in our weakness. For we do not know what to pray for as we ought, but the Spirit Himself makes intercession for us with groanings which cannot be uttered. Now He who searches the hearts knows what the mind of the Spirit is, because He makes intercession for the saints according to the will of God." (Rom. 8:26-27)

The meaning here is not that the Holy Spirit has us on His "prayer list" making us the object of His prayer. It means rather that He knows what to pray and births within the believer His burden, unfolding the content of His prayer. We then give voice to that intercession. Prayer originates within the Spirit.

The Holy Spirit is called the Spirit of grace and supplication (Zech. 12:10). He intercedes through us. All prayer is to be *"in the Spirit."* This phrase does not refer only to praying in tongues. All prayer and supplication are to be *"in the Spirit"*

(Eph. 6:18), whether that prayer is in tongues or in one's own native language. We are to pray with the provision that the Holy Spirit gives (Jude 20).

By comparing two nearly identical portions from Paul's epistles, we can see this provision. He states in Galatians 4:6 that God has sent forth the Spirit of His Son into our hearts crying "Abba, Father!" It is the Spirit that makes the cry in our hearts. In Romans 8:15, Paul declares that we, as believers, cry out "Abba, Father" because we have received the Spirit. This makes it plain that the Holy Spirit initiates the cry, but we give voice to that cry through our lips. This is the secret to intercession. We are simply the vessels through whom the Holy Spirit prays.

The Holy Spirit is referred to as the firstfruits of our salvation, while the resurrection of the body is likened to the harvest (Rom. 8:23). In other words, salvation will be complete at the return of Christ when the resurrection takes place. Nevertheless, our salvation has been set in motion and already we are the children of God. The gift of the Spirit has been granted now to train and prepare the church for the full and final inheritance she will obtain in that day. The Holy Spirit, in the interim, is God's provision for every aspect of Christian life, including prayer. The Spirit longs for that day of days to come, when all creation will be set free from corruption into the glorious liberty of the sons of God. At present, He is grieved at the state of the world and longs to reconcile creation with the Creator. This burden of the Spirit is the basis for the prayer life of the church. (Read Romans 8:14-30.)

The word "help" in Romans 8:26 is instructive. The Greek word has two prefixes, meaning "instead of" and "together with." The Holy Spirit does what we cannot do and He uses our voices. He requires our cooperation as the vessels through whom He prays.

Provision for Prayer

There is a major difference between the yearnings of the Holy Spirit within, causing us to cry out to God, and our attempts to pray in our own strength, guided by our own perceptions and wisdom. As in all areas of life, we must cease from self-effort, rest in the Lord, and allow the Spirit of God to bear witness within our spirits. Thus, it becomes obvious that a prayer life and a Spirit-filled walk go hand in hand. One is not possible without the other. A Spirit-filled walk naturally leads itself to prayer, for that is the Spirit's nature.

This should be comforting to those who have relied on their own will power, ability, wisdom, and strength. We should give ourselves to the Lord and confess our weaknesses. We can ask God to bestow upon us the grace of prayer, for this is a natural activity of the Holy Spirit that has been given to us. In childlike confidence, we wait upon God and glorify Him. We do not attempt to pray as we seek fellowship with the Father. The Holy Spirit will produce His yearnings within us.

Simply put, the performance of the will of God may be made in four statements. **Firstly**, God desires to do something. **Secondly**, He, by the Spirit, imparts that desire to His people, creating a burden. **Thirdly**, God's people utter that burden back to Him in prayer and intercession. **Fourthly**, God performs His will.

The Holy Spirit is the key ingredient in the whole process. He bears witness within our spirits concerning the mind of God. He reveals what God desires to accomplish. The longings of God are reproduced in the believer. The Holy Spirit enlightens us with wisdom and revelation, opening the eyes of our understanding (Eph. 1:17-18). Thus, we know for what to pray. The same Holy Spirit will lead us into the very presence of God (Eph. 2:18). The Holy Spirit imparts faith for the answer to be given. Faith always follows revelation (c.f. Is. 53:1). In every area, whether it is knowledge, wisdom, revelation or power in prayer, the Holy Spirit is the provision.

Provision for Prayer

Thought Questions

1. "Moreover, as for me, far be it from me that I should sin against the Lord in ceasing to pray for you; but I will teach you the good and the right way." 1 Samuel 12:23. Obviously, Samuel considered prayerlessness sin. Do you agree with Samuel? If so, explain why you think Samuel is correct.

2. "The Holy Spirit is referred to as the firstfruits of our salvation, while the resurrection of the body is likened to the harvest." Discuss this quote from the author as fully as you can.

3. Explain fully the word "help" in Rom. 8:26.

4. The performance of the will of God may be made in four statements. What are they?

Provision for Prayer (2)

Burden for Prayer

It was earlier stated that prayer is not telling God what to do; it is agreeing with God in that which He has revealed He desires to do. Prayer is not enforcing our will upon God, nor using His power to manipulate circumstances to our liking. When God desires to accomplish a certain end, He shares that desire with His people who then pray it back to Him. Then God will act. That sharing of His will, heart and mind to His people by the Spirit creates within the heart of the believer a "burden."

The entire work of God functions according to the following four principles. It needs to be emphasized that nothing happens outside of prayer.

1) If the church desires to see a lasting revival, then she must see God's eternal purpose, His blueprint for the ages. What is God doing overall? If the big picture is not appreciated, the church will be tempted to focus on the "part" that is presently being played out, to relate the work of God to itself rather than to Christ.

2) The church must also recognize that all spiritual work is initiated by God and must be Spirit-directed. In Acts 16, the Holy Spirit would not allow Paul to go into certain regions with the gospel message (Acts 16:6-9). Later, Paul was permitted to go into some of those areas.

3) Further, it must be emphasized that the work of God must be carried out in God's power and not by self-sufficiency or worldly ideas.

4) Finally, it needs to be stated that the motive must be pure, solely concerned for the glory of God and not for recognition or thrills. For example, Elijah's great concern was that the people might know that the Lord is God (1 Kgs. 18:36-37).

In each of these points, the Holy Spirit is the key. As the Holy Spirit reveals the mind and desire of God to us, reproducing His longings within us, a burden is created. The church's duty is to discharge that burden. The church is to pray until there is no more burden. Only then is the prayer finished. How God's people need to recognize that God does not act apart from the prayer of the church! Though God has all power, He does not act or move without the church's agreement in prayer. Just as the train can run only where the tracks have been laid, the power of God moves only after effective prayer has been offered.

The prophets of old spoke according to the principle of burden. Isaiah spoke of prophetic oracles as burdens. (See Is. 13:1; 15:1; 17:1; 19:1; 21:1,11,13; 22:1; 23:1.) The Hebrew word for 'burden' (massah) suggests something that is carried. Thus, a burden is something that has touched one's inner life. For example, a mother is naturally touched by the illness of her infant child. The situation naturally weighs upon her heart and mind. She does not need to be reminded of the circumstance. Similarly, the Holy Spirit's imparted burden is an inner longing that desires what God desires. That desire may be very intense and passionate or be restful and quiet. The burden may be patient or boldly lay claim to the desires of God. The Psalmist learned to wait upon God (Ps. 62:1,5). He learned to quiet his soul. The soul must be quiet to hear the voice of God.

The burden of the Lord is different from the natural cares and anxieties that tend to crush the human soul. It is different from a weight that oppresses the heart. Rather, it is the mind and heart of God, in contrast to this sinful world, being reproduced in the believer. The believer begins to yearn for that which God yearns. As God shares His desires to accomplish certain ends with His people, it creates a burden within the church for the same desire. God's people speak that burden back to Him in prayer. That is how it is released. Sometimes, if the burden is strong, fasting may be required to discharge the burden. When the burden is fully discharged, then prayer for that particular situation is finished.

Psalm 6 is an excellent example of "praying through." In the first seven verses, the Psalmist poured out his heart to God. He cried out to the Lord, "How long?" He was weary with groaning; he was consumed with grief. His enemies appeared to have the upper hand. Then, in verse 8, a remarkable change took place. Having touched God, he then spoke with a strong faith to his enemies, because he prayed through and had overcome. The Lord had heard his supplications and received his prayer. Thus, he gained boldness in the face of his enemies. He declared the victory of the Lord and was enabled to give voice to faith.

May the Lord grant the church the persistence to pray until she has prayed through, until faith has been born to receive that which God yearns to do!

Provision for Prayer

Thought Questions

1. What is a "burden from the Lord?"

2. How is this burden different from the cares of the world?

3. How does a believer get a burden?

4. How is a burden discharged?

5. "If the church desires to see a lasting revival, then she must see God's eternal purpose, His blueprint for the ages." Why is it important for the church to understand God's "blueprint for the ages?"

Provision for Prayer (3)

Spirit-Led Prayer

Tongues, Interpretation, and Prophecy

For some, the expression "Pray in the Spirit" has brought confusion. They have equated that statement with praying in tongues. This is unfortunate for, as we have seen, all prayer is to be inspired, guided, and empowered by the Spirit. When the apostle Paul refers to praying in tongues, he uses the words *"pray with the Spirit."* (1 Cor. 14:15). Scripture reveals that the Holy Spirit will lead us to pray in our mother tongue, in other tongues (glossalalia) and also with groanings that cannot be articulated. We shall examine all types of Spirit-inspired prayer. However, to grasp these comments, it would be advisable to first gain an understanding of the issues Paul was addressing with the Corinthians throughout 1 Corinthians 14, since much of the discussion will arise from there.

The Corinthians, because they had received gifts of the Spirit (especially tongues), mistakenly thought that they had arrived at the pinnacle of spirituality. They had missed the essence of true spirituality, which is love. Their excessive practice of speaking with other tongues led to a variety of abuses. One of the abuses was speaking in tongues in the public assembly without interpretation. Another abuse was disregarding the value of other gifts, such as prophecy. It appears that times have not really changed; believers down through the centuries have committed the same errors as the Corinthians.

Many people will allow emotional experiences to shape and form their doctrines rather than a proper study of the Scriptures. This holds very true in regards to tongues, interpretation, and prophecy, because these gifts (especially tongues) can produce emotional responses that can cause us to neglect proper attention to the Scriptures. 1 Corinthians 14:1-5 is worthy of careful study:

> Pursue love, and desire spiritual gifts, but especially that you may prophesy. For he who speaks in a tongue does not speak to men but to God, for no one understands him; however, in the spirit he speaks mysteries. But he who prophesies speaks edification and exhortation and comfort to men. He who speaks in a tongue edifies himself, but he who prophesies edifies the church. I wish you all spoke with tongues, but even more that you prophesied; for he who prophesies is greater than he who speaks with tongues, unless indeed he interprets, that the church may receive edification.

According to these verses, prophecy is God speaking by the Spirit to man. Tongues, on the other hand, go the other direction. By the Spirit, man speaks mysteries to God. Not tongues per se, but tongues without interpretation in the public assembly is at issue. Unintelligible utterances do not edify. Tongues when interpreted do edify. Confusion is encountered in verse 5 where some equate the combination of tongues and interpretation to prophecy. However, such a conclusion would contradict his statements in verses 2 and 3. Paul is saying that tongues with interpretation will bring edification to the church, not that it serves the same purpose.

As Paul speaks in verses 6-12, he uses analogies from everyday life to demonstrate that edification comes only from what is understood:

The Privilege of Prayer

But now, brethren, if I come to you speaking with tongues, what shall I profit you unless I speak to you either by revelation, by knowledge, by prophesying, or by teaching? Even things without life, whether flute or harp, when they make a sound, unless they make a distinction in the sounds, how will it be known what is piped or played? For if the trumpet makes an uncertain sound, who will prepare for battle? So likewise you, unless you utter by the tongue words easy to understand, how will it be known what is spoken? For you will be speaking into the air. There are, it may be, so many kinds of languages in the world, and none of them is without significance. Therefore, if I do not know the meaning of the language, I shall be a foreigner to him who speaks, and he who speaks will be a foreigner to me. Even so you, since you are zealous for spiritual gifts, let it be for the edification of the church that you seek to excel.

Thus, tongues in the assembly without interpretation serve no useful purpose. During assembly, we are to excel in edifying the church.

What are the implications of this? They are discussed in verses 13-20:

Therefore let him who speaks in a tongue pray that he may interpret. For if I pray in a tongue, my spirit prays, but my understanding is unfruitful. What is the conclusion then? I will pray with the spirit, and I will also pray with the understanding. I will sing with the spirit, and I will also

sing with the understanding. Otherwise, if you
bless with the spirit, how will he who occupies
the place of the uninformed say "Amen" at your
giving of thanks, since he does not understand
what you say? For you indeed give thanks well,
but the other is not edified. I thank my God I
speak with tongues more than you all; yet in the
church I would rather speak five words with my
understanding, that I may teach others also, than
ten thousand words in a tongue. Brethren, do not
be children in understanding; however, in malice
be babes, but in understanding be mature.

In the assembly, tongues are to be interpreted. Tongues, since
they are directed toward God, take the form of praise, prayer,
blessing, and giving thanks. It is not a message from the Lord to
the congregation. That is the function of prophecy. Thus, the
interpretation of tongues should reveal the content of the praise,
prayer, blessing, or giving of thanks. Paul does not disparage
speaking in tongues. It is simply not the best gift for the public
assembly. He would rather bring teaching.

What then is the value of tongues? Paul made unlimited use of it
in his private life, in his "prayer closet." Tongues bring edification to the one doing the praying, but that is not the goal of the
public assembly. In the assembly, corporate edification is to be
sought.

In verses 21-25, Paul again emphasizes this point:

In the law it is written: With men of other
tongues and other lips I will speak to this people;
And yet, for all that, they will not hear me, says
the Lord. Therefore tongues are for a sign, not to

those who believe but to unbelievers; but prophesying is not for unbelievers but for those who believe. Therefore if the whole church comes together in one place, and all speak with tongues,
and there come in those who are uninformed or
unbelievers, will they not say that you are out of
your mind? But if all prophesy, and an unbeliever
or an uninformed person comes in, he is con-
vinced by all, he is convicted by all. And thus the
secrets of his heart are revealed; and so, falling
down on his face, he will worship God and report
that God is truly among you.

Tongues edify when they are understood. In what sense are they
a sign to the unbeliever? The answer is, as on the day of Pentecost, when unbelievers heard the disciples speak in their dialects
(Acts 2), no interpretation was needed, for the hearer understood
them. This acted as a sign to them. However, in church, it is
prophecy that is understood; therefore, it is the best gift for edifying the church.

In what situation do tongues offend unbelievers? Obviously,
when they don't understand them, they are offended. An unbelieving visitor in a church service will think everyone is mad
who speaks such unintelligible gibberish that is foreign to him.
However, if a prophecy comes that reveals the condition of his
heart, he will acknowledge the presence of God in the midst.
Either way, what is understood edifies.

The conclusions of this discussion are put forward in verses 26-
31:

How is it then, brethren? Whenever you come together, each of you has a psalm, has a teaching,

has a tongue, has a revelation, has an interpretation. Let all things be done for edification. If anyone speaks in a tongue, let there be two or at the most three, each in turn, and let one interpret. But if there is no interpreter, let him keep silent in church, and let him speak to himself and to God. Let two or three prophets speak, and let the others judge. But if anything is revealed to another who sits by, let the first keep silent. For you can all prophesy one by one, that all may learn and all may be encouraged.

Everything that takes place in the church service should have edification as its goal. Tongues, since its primary use is for personal edification, should not be as widely used as other gifts. There is a limit of two or three utterances that should come forth. If there is no interpreter, tongues should be done quietly, under one's breath, as it were, to one's self and to God. This again emphasizes that tongues and the interpretation are both Godward. However, there is no limit to the gift of prophecy, for that is the prime vehicle of edification to the church.

The final conclusion concerning tongues is brought forward in verses 39 and 40:

Therefore, brethren, desire earnestly to prophesy and do not forbid to speak with tongues. Let all things be done decently and in order.

Paul does not forbid speaking with tongues, but wants to see them used properly so that all things are done decently and in order. The value of tongues is found in prayer and worship with countless blessings in our personal and private lives as we walk with God.

The Privilege of Prayer

Praying *in* the Spirit

> praying always with all prayer and supplication
> in the Spirit, being watchful to this end with all
> perseverance and supplication for all the saints -
> (Eph. 6:18)

> But you, beloved, building yourselves up on your
> most holy faith, praying in the Holy Spirit, (Jude
> 20)

So far, we have declared that prayer is the school and the training ground where the Body of Christ is prepared for its destiny as joint-heirs with Christ in God's eternal purpose for His Son. We have said that prayer is not telling God what to do; it is agreeing with His revealed desires. We have also stated that intercession is the ministry of the Holy Spirit; it is not the product of man's self-effort. The Spirit we have received is the Spirit of grace and supplication. We are the vessels through whom He prays.

Before God accomplishes His will, He shares that knowledge with His people. The Holy Spirit brings us revelation of God's will. He creates a desire in us for the things of God and for the will of God to be accomplished. This burden that has touched our inner life and heart is then uttered back to God in prayer. We give voice to the witness of the Holy Spirit within us. We are to pray until the whole burden is lifted. (Some things require a determined perseverance over a long period of time.) At that point we know that heaven has added its "Amen" and the thing is finished. God will then accomplish and fulfill His desire in the earth.

Provision for Prayer

Through the entire process, the Holy Spirit is the crucial ingredient that makes prayer possible. The Holy Spirit reveals the mind of God, creates the desire in us for it to be accomplished, gives the content of prayer, prays through us, and gives us the "staying power" until the burden is fully released. From beginning to end, the Holy Spirit grants the power for prayer.

As the Spirit leads us in prayer, we will find that He guides our prayer in our mother tongue, in other tongues as He gives utterance, and also with yearnings too deep for words. We shall examine all three.

Praying with our Mother Tongue

This is simply praying in one's normal language or dialect. This may be viewed through two lenses. One knows how to pray instinctively and the other is a conscious apprehension of the mind of God in a certain matter.

For certain issues, we should instinctively know the mind of God. Through constant and close fellowship with Him, we come to know His will, perspective and desires for life in general. A prayer life will develop as we grow in the knowledge of the Lord. As we allow His nature and character traits to be reproduced in us, the knowledge of His will becomes more instinctive and automatic and unconsciously passes through our lips as we take all things to God in prayer.

However, there are many matters that require discernment concerning God's heart and purpose. If someone is going through trial, is it the enemy that needs to be resisted? Perhaps, God has permitted this as a discipline. If that is true, then there is need for repentance before the enemy of our souls can be resisted. Is the person being prepared for a fuller expression of God's will

The Privilege of Prayer

for his life? Can Satan be blamed for financial difficulties if a person doesn't know how to budget properly, or spends foolishly on his own appetites? Obviously, to pray accurately, one must have the discernment of the Holy Spirit.

Another aspect needs to be made clear. The Spirit of God directs the work of God. The work of the ministry is not done arbitrarily. God directs His own work. Where does God want any given worker to minister at any given time? Why go to Africa when God has work ready in Australia? The place to carry out that will needs to be revealed. The timing of doing the will of God needs to be ascertained. What is the message that will be delivered? Answers to questions like these need to be consciously apprehended by the Spirit.

When the Holy Spirit gives specific directions for issues like these, the burden for it is laid upon our hearts. Having discerned the will of God for a certain area, we follow it with a conscious season of prayer until that burden is discharged. The awareness of the will of God is carried within until it is totally released back to God in prayer. It should go without saying that praying requires one to be in fellowship with God so that as we wait upon Him opportunity is provided for Him to speak to us.

The mercy seat in the Tabernacle was a place of fellowship with God. There, God communed with Moses (Ex. 25:22), giving him instructions and directions for His people. The Psalmist instructed his own soul to wait upon God, for his expectation came from Him (Ps. 62:1,5). In another place, God commands us to "be still" and know that He is God. (Ps. 46:10) The Christian life is one in which the Lord dines with us and we with Him (Rev. 3:20). If Moses had not turned aside to see the burning bush, would he have missed God's call for his life (Ex. 3:2-4)?

Provision for Prayer

There is no doubt that we must develop the habit of being alone with God to digest Scripture, absorb revelation, meditate upon His Word, worship and praise Him, and be quiet before Him so that we may hear His voice and discern His will. Then we can utter that will back to God in prayer, consciously understanding the burden and praying with the mind and with intelligence concerning the fulfillment of God's wishes and desires.

Praying *with* the Spirit

1 Corinthians 14:15-16 speaks of praying and blessing with the Spirit. This is the only passage in Scripture that uses the term, "*with* the Spirit," not "*in* the Spirit." This refers specifically to the use of speaking with tongues in prayer and worship. As mentioned previously, Paul was correcting misunderstandings of tongues and spirituality. Speaking with tongues is to enable the believer, by the aid of the Holy Spirit, to speak toward God. Prophecy, also given by the Holy Spirit, is spoken toward man (1 Cor. 14:2-3). Speaking in tongues is giving vent to praise, worship, thanksgiving and prayer toward God. Since this is the case, speaking with other tongues has invaluable use in one's own private life. This is the meaning of Paul's statements in 1 Corinthians 14:18,19. In the public assembly, prophecy is preferred because the aim is to edify the whole congregation, not just one's self. However, there is unlimited use for tongues in the privacy of one's own devotions as evidenced by Paul's testimony.

There are times in praying when, even after consciously apprehending the mind of God, praying with one's natural tongue is insufficient to release the burden. Praying with tongues will assist in lifting the burden. There will be a knowing within the believer that this is more than praise, an intensification of intercession. As the Holy Spirit inspires the tongues, the prayer becomes more detailed and specific.

Often in our walk with the Lord, there are numerous issues that are beyond our grasp. We certainly cannot see all that the Lord sees, nor understand all that He does and permits. We walk and live by faith, many times trusting His character in the absence of a specific "word" from Him. Praying with other tongues enables us to sympathize with God in spite of our shortcomings when it comes to our own eternity. Our finite minds cannot grasp the full mysteries of God, but by praying with other tongues we are enabled to identify with the counsels of God. Thus, by praying with other tongues, the God-given burden is uttered back to God for Him to perform His will.

There also may be times when the Spirit leads in prayer this way because it is better if we do not know all the facts concerning the situations and people involved in our prayer.

Praying with Groanings

There are times when the desires of God are felt very deeply within the spirit of the believer. The yearnings become too deep for expression with words, whether in one's mother tongue or even with other tongues. The burden simply is not released. Paul speaks of this in Romans 8:19-27. All creation yearns deeply for deliverance from its present state of vanity into the glorious liberty that it shall experience when the sons of God are manifested. The Holy Spirit creates the same sense in the believer, who already experiences the firstfruits of this glorious salvation.

Just as God is moving all things toward the ultimate realization of His eternal purpose, the Holy Spirit yearns for its completion. He brings a sense within the believer that God will bring all things to their conclusion, and all will be brought into perfect harmony with the glory of God. Deep in the heart of the believer is a longing for salvation to come to its consummation. This intense desire for the will of God to be completed issues forth in prayer. Out of the well of one's inner being come groanings, sighs and weeping as if the heart would break. Sometimes, the only words that come forth are "O God."

Many times this type of praying in the Spirit occurs when one is in intercession for people in deep trial, for something major, or for something that may take years to accomplish.

When Jesus was in the garden of Gethsemane, He prayed more earnestly and His sweat became as if it were great drops of blood falling to the ground (Lk. 22:44). The writer of Hebrews mentions this, describing the prayer of Christ as with vehement cries and tears. The prayer of Christ was answered because He "feared" or reverenced His Father, willing only to do His will (Heb. 5:7).

This prayer life is to be the norm for the New Testament church. Just as Christ agonized in prayer in the Garden, Epaphras, a servant of Christ, *"labored"* fervently in prayer so that the saints would stand perfect and complete in all the will of God (Col 4:12). Paul asked the Roman believers to *"strive"* together in prayer for him: that he would be delivered from the hands of unbelievers, that his service to the poor of Jerusalem would be accepted, and that he would be able to get to Rome (Rom. 15:30-32). The Holy Spirit will likewise give us an earnest fervency in prayer, wholeheartedly sympathizing with the will of God in all things.

Praying with Fastings

There are times when burdens need to be assisted with fasting. Man is not to live by bread alone (Matt. 4:4): he is to live by the Word of God. There are times when the Word of the Lord is not being heard and a person may need to set himself apart to be alone with God. Often when new direction is coming into a person's life, he may sense the Lord leading him apart for a season. Often fasting will be done when a burden from the Lord is intense. We fast to loose the bands of wickedness, to undo the heavy burdens, to let the oppressed go free, and to break every yoke, to share bread with the hungry, to bring the poor to our house, to cover the naked, and not to hide ourselves from our own flesh (Is. 58:6-7).

The apostle Paul is an example of a man of prayer. He prayed with understanding. His epistles almost always begin with a prayer, showing that he instinctively knew the mind of God (Eph. 1:15-19). Paul prayed with tongues more than the Corinthians, and that was quite a boast (1 Cor. 14:18). Paul found himself in labor for others, that Christ be formed in them (Gal. 4:19). He often experienced sleepless nights and fasted frequently (2 Cor. 11:27). Paul had his habits of prayer, but in addition, he prayed when the Spirit called him apart.

Does not the church need to regain this fervency in prayer? May God raise up prayer warriors who labor in intercession, striving in prayer for the will of God to be accomplished. We must appreciate that God's will is done after it first passes through the church in prayer. The church is to discharge the burden of the Spirit in the strength of the Spirit. May God grant that the church once again gives voice to the Spirit's intercession!

Provision for Prayer

Thought Questions

1. Explain the difference between these two terms "Pray *in* the Spirit" and "Pray *with* the Spirit."

2. Discuss the difference between praying in one's mother tongue, with other tongues, and with groanings that cannot be uttered.

3. Why is fasting sometimes required to discharge a prayer burden?

Section Four

Power by Prayer

Section Four

Power by Prayer (1)

Prayer and the Work of God

When Jesus spoke with His disciples just before He was betrayed, He told of many changes that were about to take place. The disciples would have difficulty understanding many of these. One of the lessons the Lord intended to impress upon those who had followed Him was the place and necessity of prayer. Jesus would be physically removed from them, and they were then to approach the Father in His name.

> Most assuredly, I say to you, he who believes in Me, the works that I do he will do also; and greater works than these he will do, because I go to My Father. And whatever you ask in My name, that I will do, that the Father may be glorified in the Son. If you ask anything in My name, I will do it. (Jn. 14:12-14)

> If you abide in Me, and My words abide in you, you will ask what you desire, and it shall be done for you. (Jn. 15:7)

> You did not choose Me, but I chose you and appointed you that you should go and bear fruit, and that your fruit should remain, that whatever you ask the Father in My name He may give you. (Jn. 15:16)

> And in that day you will ask Me nothing. Most assuredly, I say to you, whatever you ask the Father in My name He will give you. Until now you have asked nothing in My name. Ask, and you will receive, that your joy may be full. (Jn. 16:23-24)

> In that day you will ask in My name, and I do not say to you that I shall pray the Father for you; for the Father Himself loves you, because you have loved Me, and have believed that I came forth from God. (Jn. 16:26-27)

This teaching of Jesus declares that the work of the ministry is to be carried out through prayer. Prayer is the manner through which all the will of God will be accomplished. Jesus spoke much about the ministry of the Holy Spirit in the same chapters of Scripture, and the whole of the New Testament bears witness to the fact that the work of the Spirit is given in response to persevering, believing, and Spirit-directed prayer (Lk. 11:9-13).

The New Testament emphasizes that prayer must be the first function of the church. Paul urged the young Thessalonian church to pray without ceasing (1 Thess. 5:17). This refers to specific times of prayer as well as continuous, unbroken fellowship with God. The Holy Spirit dwells within, making our relationship with Him both functional and practical.

Paul had left young Timothy in Ephesus to set in order certain things in the life of the church. Without apology, he instructed that prayer is to have first place in the daily life of the church (1 Tim. 2:1). By contrast, most often the prayer meeting is the least attended of all the church functions and it is relegated to a midweek gathering. Nevertheless, the primary responsibility of the church is to make intercessions, supplications, prayers, and to give thanks. It is the duty of men everywhere to lift up holy hands without wrath and doubting (1 Tim. 2:8). Likewise, the women in presenting themselves properly are to pray also (1 Tim. 2:9). Through prayer and the Word of God, everything is set aside for use and is sanctified (1 Tim. 4:4-5). Paul makes it clear that those who have been entrusted with time are to invest that time with supplications night and day, and he has much to say to those who abuse that freedom (1 Tim. 5:3-5, 11-13).

There are times when the call to prayer requires the laying aside of other responsibilities. Marriage partners may need to consent to set aside normal sexual relationships for the purpose of giving themselves over to prayer (1 Cor. 7:5). The church is to "continue steadfastly" in prayer (Rom. 12:12). We are instructed to continue earnestly in prayer and watch in the same with thanksgiving (Col. 4:2). This means to devote one's self to prayer. We are also exhorted to pray in the Spirit always (Eph. 6:18). Diligence to prayer should be the normal lifestyle of the church.

The power of the Holy Spirit moves in response to prayer. Luke, who records this truth (Lk. 11:9-13), gives ample testimony throughout the Book of Acts. Before the day of Pentecost, upon which the Spirit fell, one hundred and twenty continued with one accord in prayer and supplication (Acts 1:14). The converts on that day adopted a lifestyle of continuing in prayer (Acts 2:42). The miracle of the lame man healed as Peter and John were going to the temple occurred as they were on the way to the hour of prayer (Acts 3:1). The early church agreed together in prayer for miracles to take place. This was the reason for the church's overcoming power and testimony (Acts 4:24-31).

The apostles did not allow infringement upon their time for prayer and the Word of God. They set others over the administration duties so they might give themselves continually to prayer and the Word of God (Acts 6:2-4).

Immediately upon conversion, Saul of Tarsus sought the Lord with three days of fasting (Acts 9:9). Cornelius was a devout man, and prayed to God always (Acts 10:2). Peter's custom was to separate himself for prayer (Acts 10:9). Earnest and fervent prayer was offered on behalf of the apostle Peter when Herod had imprisoned him. This prayer was without ceasing and many people were gathered together to pray (Acts 12:5,12). The leaders of the church of Antioch recognized that their first responsibility was to minister not unto men, but unto the Lord. This they did by fasting (Acts 13:1-3). Fellowship with God must precede God's work!

The choice of elders was made only in the context of prayer and fasting (Acts 14:23). A place and time had been set aside for prayer; this was the normal custom (Acts 16:13). The apostles followed this pattern (Acts 16:16). Even the prison house became an opportunity for prayer and praise (Acts 16:25). Paul took advantage of the time in prison: he was separated unto prayer!

When taking leave of beloved believers, Paul prayed with them (Acts 20:36; 21:5). Thus, both direction and blessing were granted. The apostle Paul was definitely a man of prayer (Acts 22:17). Prayer was the factor that moved the miraculous power of the Holy Spirit. It seemed as if the early church understood that it could, like Jesus, function in kingly power only because it first acted as a priest in prayer (Heb. 7:25).

In the New Testament, one Greek word is used constantly in connection with prayer. "Proskartereo" is found in the following verses. We will give ourselves continually to prayer (Acts 6:4).

The Privilege of Prayer

Continuing instant in prayer (Rom. 12:12). Continue earnestly in prayer (Col. 4:2). And they continued steadfastly … in prayers (Acts 2:42).

The following words may be used to illustrate the meaning of this Greek word "proskartereo:" earnest, fervent, perseverant, and diligent. The only other context in which Paul used this word was when he described the diligence the government had in collecting taxes (Rom. 13:6)!

May the Lord grant that the church takes up this glorious privilege of prayer.

Power by Prayer

Thought Questions

1. The New Testament emphasizes that prayer must be the first function of the church. Has that been your church experience? If not, what do you think are the reasons for prayerlessness in the church generally? If you have not seen much evidence of the Holy Spirit's involvement in the lives of church members, what may be the solution to this situation?

2. As you studied this book, you read several accounts of the positive consequences of fervent prayer. In addition, you may have read the Book of Acts recently. List all the events you can that were the results of effective prayer.

Power by Prayer (2)

Paul's Requests for Prayer

Reading through the Book of Acts, we cannot help but marvel at the great moves of the Holy Spirit. Wonder holds us captive as we read of prison doors opening of their own accord, earthquakes loosing chains from prisoners, miraculous healings and deliverances, people being filled with the Holy Spirit, and entire cities being turned upside down (perhaps, right side up is a more accurate expression) by the gospel of Jesus Christ. Though there was much opposition, the church emerged triumphant as the power of the Holy Spirit directed and energized its activities.

The Book of Acts records the highlights of the ministry of the Holy Spirit. It lays out for us the story of the Church as it is visible to the natural eye. In reality, the Book of Acts only gives a fragmented view of the early church's history. Luke only records the events that are in accord with his purpose of writing. (For example, note that Titus is not even mentioned in the Acts, even though we learn from the epistles that he was an integral part of Paul's team of workers.) To go behind the scenes, we must go to the epistles. While Acts speaks of the trials and ensuing triumphs, the epistles show us what transpired in the lives of both the apostles and the local churches that led to those victories.

In the stories referred to, Paul, as on many occasions, requested prayer for himself. The unobserved prayer of the church gave Paul and the other apostles the great victories that are recorded for us in the Book of Acts. As we will see in Paul's example, it was the Spirit-filled, persevering prayer of the churches on his behalf (for which he continually asked) that won the victories, brought the demonstrations of power, strengthened the feeble, gave boldness and wrought strength and character in the lives of the men and women of God. These were all possible because of the intercession of the saints!

Often we look at our favorite Bible heroes as super giants of the faith and tend to forget that while they indeed made great strides with God, they were also men and women of the same nature as ourselves (Acts 14:25; James 5:17). Similar to our experience, they came up against weariness and depression. Even Elijah desired that his life would end (1 Kgs. 19:4). Paul experienced anxiety and fear (2 Cor. 7:5). Let us ever be mindful that God puts his treasure in earthen vessels, that the excellency of the power may be of God and not of us (2 Cor. 4:7).

It was out of this realization that Paul, not thinking of himself more highly than he ought, continuously asked for intercession to be made on his behalf. Let us now look at these requests by the apostle and see how the believing petitioning of the church made the victories possible.

Brethren, pray for us. (1 Thess. 5:25)

Paul knew the secret for success - effective prayer. Great persecution had driven Paul out of the city of Thessalonica (Acts 17:1-15). He was unable to return, though he was very anxious concerning the welfare of the saints there. Not only had the unbelieving Jews driven him from Thessalonica, but also they pursued him and forced him out of Berea as well. He was praying night and day that he might see the infant church again, finish what he had begun, and perfect that which was lacking in their faith (1 Thess. 3:10). Paul requested prayer, trusting that God would give him strength and the ability to do God's will, and that He would ensure the success of the apostolic work.

The Privilege of Prayer

**Finally, brethren, pray for us, that the word of
the Lord may run swiftly and be glorified, just
as it is with you, and that we may be delivered
from unreasonable and wicked men; for not
all have faith.** (2 Thess. 3:1-2)

Paul may be quoting Psalm 147:15 in this petition for prayer,
where it states that God's Word runs very swiftly. For the gospel
to run swiftly means that it may be preached freely and unim-
peded and that all obstacles to it may be removed. Paul is in the
city of Corinth when he makes this request.

Paul's experience there is recorded in Acts 18:1-18. He had been
reasoning in the synagogue every Sabbath and was persuading
both Jews and Greeks. Being pressed in his spirit, he testified to
the Jews that Jesus indeed was the Messiah for which they
looked. However, he met with a violent reaction which he de-
scribes in 1 Thessalonians 2:14-16, stating that the apostolic
party was being persecuted, and that they were being charged
not to preach to the Gentiles that they might be saved. Paul
asked for prayer that the Word of the Lord might have free
course (run swiftly). He had come up against stubborn unbelievers who would not listen to logic or debate.

The city of Corinth was known as a wicked city with every sort
of vice found there. It desperately needed the gospel of Christ.
Paul's request that the Word may be glorified is a request that it
would produce many converts (c.f. Acts 13:48).

Paul had asked that he would be delivered from unreasonable
and wicked men. When Gallio was deputy, the Jews once again
made insurrection against Paul. The answer to Paul's request is
seen in the fact that he was able to spend eighteen months in the
city of Corinth reaping a harvest of souls. In response to the

82

prayers of the saints, Paul received a vision from the Lord encouraging him with a promise of protection while he worked in the city.

> **For we do not want you to be ignorant, brethren, of our trouble which came to us in Asia: that we were burdened beyond measure, above strength, so that we despaired even of life. Yes, we had the sentence of death in ourselves, that we should not trust in ourselves but in God who raises the dead, who delivered us from so great a death, and does deliver us; in whom we trust that he will still deliver us, you also helping together in prayer for us, that thanks may be given by many persons on our behalf for the gift granted to us through many.**
> (2 Cor. 1:8-11)

The last portion of the above passage is better understood when it is stated this way: The people who prayed will show great gratitude when they realize that God answered their prayers for Paul. The difficult and hazardous time to which Paul refers in this passage is the riot at Ephesus recorded in Acts 19:24-41. The entire city was in an uproar in an attempt to rid the city of the gospel workers. The lives of Paul and the other workers were in grave danger. Priscilla and Aquila were with Paul at this time and they had risked their lives as well (Rom. 16:3-4). Paul makes it clear that it was the prayers of the saints that saved his life and brought him through a situation that was beyond his ability to cope, both physically and mentally.

> **Now I beg you, brethren, through the Lord Jesus Christ, and through the love of the Spirit, that you strive together with me in prayers to**

The Privilege of Prayer

God for me, that I may be delivered from those in Judea who do not believe, and that my service for Jerusalem may be acceptable to the saints, that I may come to you with joy by the will of God, and may be refreshed together with you. (Rom. 15:30-32)

Paul asked the saints to "strive" together with him in prayer. The same Greek word was translated "to agonize" when Jesus prayed in the Garden of Gethsemane. To help build a bridge between Jewish and Gentile believers, Paul had for some time been receiving a collection from Gentile churches for the poor believers in the Jerusalem church. The apostle asked that the way be paved with prayer, for the Jerusalem church was still greatly influenced by the Pharisees. At this point in history, Jewish converts to Christianity were considered as a sect within Judaism. Therefore, those in Jerusalem did not always appreciate Paul's message of grace and deliverance from the law. In addition to believing Jews who were still entangled in legalism, there were unbelieving Jews holding to the doctrines of the Pharisees. Paul had received many warnings about going to Jerusalem (Acts 20:22; 21:4,10-14), but he was willing to give his life if his brethren according to the flesh could be saved (Rom. 9:1-3; 10:1). Paul asked that the saints at Jerusalem accept the offering from the Gentile churches and that it would help build trust and relationship.

He also asked that he would be delivered from the unbelieving Jews upon his arrival there. The Holy Spirit forewarned the apostle that his life would be in constant danger. After the leaders in Jerusalem accepted the offering, unbelieving Jews stirred up the people, laid hold of Paul, and began to beat him with the intention of killing him. (See Acts 21:27-32; 22:22; 23:12). Only by the swift action of the Roman army was his life saved. This

Power by Prayer

was in answer to the saints striving together with Paul in prayer for him. His life was constantly in danger.

Paul had also asked that God would allow him to go to Rome. He had never been there (Rom. 1:9-13; 15:22-25,32). It is the grace of God that allows us to travel from place to place.

> **But, meanwhile, also prepare a guest room for me, for I trust that through your prayers I shall be granted to you.** (Philemon 22)

A portion of the Colossian church met at Philemon's house. Paul wrote this epistle from a Roman prison. Though the possibility of execution existed, Paul was confident that he would be released because of the prayers of the church on his behalf. While Peter was delivered from prison in a miraculous manner (Acts 12:5-7), Paul was set free by a favorable judicial decision. Paul expected the unseen Holy Spirit to exert His influence in the legal system.

> **Continue earnestly in prayer, being vigilant in it with thanksgiving; meanwhile praying also for us, that God would open to us a door for the word, to speak the mysteries of Christ, for which I am also in chains, that I may make it manifest, as I ought to speak.** (Col. 4:2-4)

This request also came while Paul was in prison. It reveals Paul's belief that prayer opens doors for ministry. Opportunities to speak and testify come as a result of prayer. Hearts, such as Lydia's (Acts 16:14), are prepared to receive because of prayer (see 1 Cor. 16:8-9; 2 Cor. 2:12; 1Thess. 1:9; 2:1; Acts 14:27).

**praying always with all prayer and supplica-
tion in the Spirit, being watchful to this end
with all perseverance and supplication for all
the saints – and for me, that utterance may be
given to me, that I may open my mouth boldly
to make known the mystery of the gospel, for
which I am an ambassador in chains; that in it
I may speak boldly, as I ought to speak.** (Eph.
6:18-20)

This request was made at the same time as that in Colossians. To
watch your prayer life is to defend it. Although Paul had been
preaching for twenty years by this time, he asked that utterance
be given to him. This shows that the ministry is a gift and does
not function by natural talent. Continuous anointing to preach
and to walk in the demonstration of the power of the Holy Spirit
comes as a result of continuous waiting upon the God. It is the
result of prayer. Paul testifies that preaching is in itself a gift
from God and a demonstration of the Holy Spirit. (See 1 Cor.
2:1-5.)

**For I know that this will turn out for my de-
liverance through your prayer and the supply
of the Spirit of Jesus Christ, according to my
earnest expectation and hope that in nothing I
shall be ashamed, but with all boldness, as always, so now also Christ will be magnified in
my body, whether by life or by death.** (Phil.
1:19-20)

This request was made during the same imprisonment, but after
a change in Roman authority created a less favorable climate for
Paul. He testifies that through their prayer, he received boldness
and strength of character. The Spirit was supplied to him. Again,

Paul was delivered from possible execution at this time and was released from prison because of prayer.

Let us note some of the answers to prayer that Paul experienced. In Philippians 4:22, Paul mentions that there were converts in Caesar's household! In Philippians 1:12-14, he declares that the surrounding heathens were being evangelized. Acts 28:16-31 is ample evidence that God allowed him great opportunity to preach the gospel, even while a prisoner. God surely answered prayer.

The Privilege of Prayer

Thought Questions

1. Paul not only taught the concept of continuous prayer but also made it part of his life. Why do you think Paul repeatedly asked churches to pray for him? For what did he seek prayer?

2. Read 2 Corinthians 1:8-11 and Acts 19:24-41. Imagine that you were in Paul's situation and enduring his discomforts and needs, fears and other emotions. Describe what your thoughts were as you went through this exercise. How did the prayers of the saints help him?

Section Five

Perseverance in Prayer

Section Five

Perseverance in Prayer (1)

A Friend at Midnight

In response to a request from His disciples to teach them how to pray, Jesus gave them an example commonly known today as "The Lord's Prayer" (Lk. 11:1-4). He immediately followed this with a parable that emphasized the necessity of persevering prayer. After giving them topics for prayer, he stressed the need for "persistence." It is the delight of God to answer prayer. However, Jesus explained that it is still necessary to persevere in prayer, to ask and to keep asking.

This parable reveals the elements of intercession, instructing us how we may be more fruitful and successful in prayer.

> And He said to them, "Which of you shall have a friend, and go to him at midnight and say to him, 'Friend, lend me three loaves; for a friend of mine has come to me on his journey, and I have nothing to set before him'; and he will answer from within and say, 'Do not trouble me; for the door is now shut, and my children are with me in bed; I cannot rise and give to you'? I say to you, though he will not rise and give to him because he is his friend, yet because of his persistence he will rise and give him as many as he needs. So I say to you, ask, and it will be given to you; seek, and you will find; knock, and it will be opened to you. For everyone who asks receives, and he who seeks finds, and to him who knocks it will be

opened. If a son asks for bread from any father among you, will he give him a stone? Or if he asks for a fish, will he give him a serpent instead of a fish? Or if he asks for an egg, will he offer him a scorpion? If you then, being evil, know how to give good gifts to your children, how much more will your heavenly Father give the Holy spirit to those who ask Him!" (Lk. 11:5-13)

Perhaps there are six discernable lessons that can be learned from this parable. They are:

1) **Sensing the need** – It is the midnight hour, a difficult time, when the needs are felt the most. The intercessor is moved by the burden.

2) **Love** – Love moves us to action. According to 1 Corinthians 13:5, love seeks not its own, forgets itself for the sake of others, takes the needs of others and makes them its own. Love compels us to prayer.

3) **Impotence** – This is most important. Impotence underscores the need for waiting on God. In and of ourselves, we have absolutely nothing to offer that can help. Only the Holy Spirit can minister to the needs. How can we trust the Holy Spirit if we are full of self-reliance? Jesus said that it is the Spirit that quickens; the flesh profits nothing (Jn. 6:63). If we realize this, then intercession is our only hope. We go to seek help. Only a word from heaven, a fresh witness of the Holy Spirit, and the immediate tangible presence of God can heal the situation. It is beyond our ability. We are powerless to help. We must remember that spiritual work is not our ministering on behalf of the Lord, but rather it is the Holy Spirit

flowing through yielded vessels. Our sense of impotence becomes the fervency of our intercession. Love compels us and our impotence drives us to earnestness so that love will not fail in its task.

4) **Faith** – Faith says, "What I don't have, a friend of mine has!" I can meet my friend's need, if I go on his behalf to the one who has all the supply. Through prayer his needs can be supplied. Does not the scripture teach that God will supply all our needs according to His riches in glory by Christ Jesus (Phil. 4:19)? All the silver and gold are His (Haggai 2:8). The earth and the fullness thereof, the world and all that dwell therein are His (Ps. 24:1).

5) **Importunity** – In this parable, the supplicant meets an unexpected denial; yet, he refuses to accept the denial as the will of his friend. Love for the one in need will persist until it wins. Importunity is shameless. It boldly continues to press in the face of denial. "I have a friend in need. What I ask is not for my own lusts. You have the abundance to meet that need. I am your friend." Importunity is faith shamelessly continuing to ask: it is trust in the character of God in spite of the apparent refusal.

6) **Reward** – Disappointment is impossible if we persevere in full assurance. We are to look at the reward and to ask and to keep on asking. Revival comes this way. Jesus teaches that the Holy Spirit is given to those who ask the Father in this manner (Lk. 11:13).

After Jesus gave this parable, He used the metaphors of asking, seeking, and knocking to describe persevering prayer. The reason for the apparent delay in answering prayer is discovered. The point Jesus is making is that God is not at all like this friend

Perseverance in Prayer

who is already in bed and unwilling to supply the need. If evil people can give good gifts, how much more will our heavenly Father who desires to give the Holy Spirit?

In using the terms ask, seek, and knock, Jesus is indicating a heightening in intensity. Each metaphor is stronger than the previous one. There is a gradation of urgency. Grammatically, these verbs are all in the continuous tense, meaning that we are to ask and to keep on asking. We are to seek and to keep on seeking; we are to knock and to keep on knocking. The meaning of these terms comes into focus when they are studied in the parallel passage found in Matthew 7:7-11 and in the context of the entire "Sermon on the Mount." Then it becomes clear why importunity is needed in prayer.

The themes of asking, seeking, and knocking are progressively revealed throughout the Sermon on the Mount. Jesus speaks of asking in Matthew 6:8. There the concern is for things and needs. As the Sermon continues, Jesus comments on how the heart needs to be free from concern over things and needs and progresses to the thought of seeking in Matthew 6:32-33. As we press forward in prayer, our focus shifts from material needs to the Kingdom of God and His righteousness. Fellowship with God and personal holiness have entered our plea to God. Then Jesus, in Matthew 7:13-14, speaks of a gate that is narrow through which one must enter. This is entrance into the kingdom of heaven where the concern is the accomplishment of the will of God (Matt. 7:21). It is a concern to do things for the glory of God.

Thus, there is a progression from desire or concern for things to yearning for righteousness and the kingdom of God. Importunity in prayer then moves us on, as we press into the kingdom and see the will of God accomplished for His honor and glory. This is the reason behind the apparent unwillingness of God to answer.

God, who is good, is more willing to answer than we are to receive. The same principle is in operation when one receives a prophetic word. When the word of the Lord is spoken to someone concerning God's will for his or her life, it is often God's goal that is being spoken, not necessarily the individual's present condition. Between the time of the prophetic word and its fulfillment, a maturing process, designed to enable the person to walk out God's revealed will, is applied. Many years may elapse from the public calling of God, witnessed by a prophetic word, to its realization.

So it is with prayer. The Holy Spirit will grant a burden of prayer for something that God intends to do. We are simply not prepared to see the answer because we often will pray selfishly with our own interests in mind. If God did answer all our prayers immediately, we could not handle the answers. As James stated, we would consume it upon our own pleasures (James 4:3). We need to be brought to the place where our only concern is the glory of God without any trace of self-interest. Importunity in prayer puts us into the position where the answer to prayer brings glory to God alone for the accomplishment of His will.

Therefore, we cannot be lazy and quit praying because the answer does not come immediately. If God has granted the burden, then it is His intention to answer the cries of His people who utter it back to Him in prayer. Thus, we must not say within ourselves that it must not be the will of God when the answer does not come easily. If we are Spirit-led in prayer, we must pray until we obtain.

Perseverance in Prayer

Jesus taught that such importunity is considered a great expression of faith. God is drawing out of us a full confession of trust in Him. The Lord commended the Canaanite woman for her persistence, and used her as an example of great faith (Matt. 15:21-28). Both she and the Roman centurion (Lk. 7:1-10) took positions of humility when they exercised great faith.

The will of God, having been revealed to us by the Holy Spirit, is to be pursued in prayer until we obtain an inner witness, until faith is imparted into our inner man. This witness may come the first time we pray, the second time or the hundredth time. Faith is not ashamed to keep on asking, seeking, and knocking. Faith is trust in the character of God. God intends to answer all Spirit-led prayer. We are to keep on praying until we know that heaven has added its "Amen."

In the context of persevering prayer, we understand the meaning of "watch and pray." The "watch" in prayer means to be alert, to collect all our faculties, and to be on our guard against intrusion. We are not to let our prayer time be spoiled.

We are to watch and pray, lest the flesh lets us fall into temptation (Matt. 26:41; Mk. 14:38). We need to watch and pray, for we do not know the time of the Lord's return (Mk. 13:32-34). It is those who watch and pray who will be counted worthy to escape the snares of the world and to stand before the Son of man (Lk. 21:34-36). Indeed, let us continue in prayer, and watch in the same with thanksgiving (Col. 4:2). It is our privilege to pray always with all prayer and supplication in the Spirit and watch thereunto with all perseverance for all saints (Eph. 6:18). Some burdens are discharged immediately, some after several times of prayer, some after a season of fasting, and others after years of intercession. To watch and pray means to ensure that we pray to the end of the matter and allow nothing to remove us from prayer.

Isaiah said it well when he wrote in Isaiah 62:6-7:

> I have set watchmen on your walls, O Jerusalem;
> They shall never hold their peace day or night.
> You who make mention of the Lord, do not keep
> silent, And give Him no rest till He establishes
> And till He makes Jerusalem a praise in the earth.

Perseverance in Prayer

Thought Questions

1. Read the parable "The Friend at Midnight;" then, discuss how the words "impotence" and "importunity" can
   be used in considering the lessons the parable teaches.

2. Describe the heightening of the terms "ask," "seek" and
   "knock."

3. Why does God often speak promises to an individual that
   are still many years from fulfillment?

4. What does it mean to be "watchful" in prayer?

Perseverance in Prayer (2)

A Widow and an Unjust Judge

Jesus taught the need for perseverance in prayer on more than one occasion. He had already spoken of a friend asking for bread at midnight (Lk. 11:5-13). Now, He gives another parable to teach that we are to pray always, and not faint. It is the story of a widow and an unjust judge as recounted by Luke:

> Then He spoke a parable to them, that men always ought to pray and not to lose heart, saying, "There was in a certain city a judge who did not fear God nor regard man. Now there was a widow in that city; and she came to him, saying, 'Get justice for me from my adversary.' And he would not for a while; but afterward he said within himself, 'Though I do not fear God nor regard man, yet because this widow troubles me I will avenge her, lest by her continual coming she weary me.' " Then the Lord said, "Hear what the unjust judge said. And shall God not avenge His own elect who cry out day and night to Him, though He bears long with them? I tell you that He will avenge them speedily. Nevertheless, when the Son of Man comes, will He really find faith on the earth?" (Lk. 18:1-8)

Here, once again, Jesus is emphasizing the need to persevere and to use importunity in prayer. To speak of the need to cry "day and night" to God, to "continually come" before Him, the Lord tells this parable. It may appear that God is withholding the answer, but real faith will not be disappointed. Faith knows that every prayer has influence in heaven and is stored up to work an

Perseverance in Prayer

answer in due time to him that perseveres to the end. To those who do persevere, the answer will come forth speedily.

Why is importunity needed with God? If He is so willing to give, why does He demand that we cry day and night? Why must we continually come before Him? Why must we be persistent and determined? When attacked by the adversary, why must we wait for God to avenge us before He acts speedily?

Notice that when the adversary attacks us, prayer is not to be directed at the adversary, but to God. Far too often believers spend more time rebuking the devil than talking to God! This is not what Jesus is teaching in the parable. Rather, He is teaching to take the case to God.

The reason Jesus gives for the delayed answer to prayer is because God is bearing long with the petitioner. He is longsuffering toward him. What can this mean? Even though the farmer longs for the crop he has planted to come forth, he knows that it must have its full season of sun and rain. Thus, he waits patiently. When God gives a burden for prayer, the praying individual (or church) is not in the position to receive the answer. He must grow and develop to the point where his faith is ripened, enabling him to both take and keep the blessing of God. Even though a father longs for his child to come home from school, he waits for the long training time to be completed.

The difficulty is not on God's side: it is altogether in us. The problem is not God's love or power, but our incapacity to receive. The fact is that we are not spiritually prepared to receive what God wants to grant. God's wisdom, righteousness and love do not grant what would harm us. Our faith must be prepared and enabled to receive for God's glory what He has revealed that He desires to give.

Even natural parents can understand this principle. We may want to give our children an inheritance while they are young in life to get them started and enabled to live better lives. We have even told them so. Yet no one would hand over any sizable amount of money if they were not first trained in handling it. Money quickly and easily received will quickly go. It will be consumed for momentary pleasures instead of laying a strong foundation for life. Before the inheritance will be given over, lessons in patience, priorities, and purpose must be learned. A wise parent, no matter how loving and willing he or she may be, will delay the gift until it is likely to be used wisely. The parent is longsuffering toward the child, bearing long with him.

It is possible that we pray according to the will of God, but from wrong motives. If God granted someone a healing ministry with signs and wonders, would it become an occasion for pride? Would a person develop a sense of self-importance? Maybe, he will begin to think he is God's answer to the world. The gift can be misused to draw attention to one's self. Miracle meetings receive big offerings! Will it become a means of financial self-preservation? While the call of God burns within the heart, it is much wiser for God to prepare the person for it. The importunity by which we cry to God is the very tool He uses to change us so we can receive.

On the one hand, God has granted burden for prayer. On the other hand, our lack of preparation becomes a barrier both to us and to God so that He cannot immediately give. This barrier has to be overcome, and that will be accomplished through our importunity in asking. We have to break through the barrier of sin in ourselves. This is what makes the striving and conflict of prayer a reality. There are obstacles to overcome. There is an adversary that attacks who needs to be avenged. As we plead with God for the adversary's removal, the persevering attitude of prayer brings those praying into a state of brokenness, of complete resignation to God, of union with His will, and of faith that can take hold of Him. In so persevering, the adversary and the obstacles in the believer are removed. Through praying to God, the obstacles in the heavens are conquered, while at the same time God conquers the intercessors. As we prevail with God, He prevails with us.

The Privilege of Prayer

Thought Questions

1. Why did Jesus teach the parable of the widow and unjust judge?

2. God bears long with the petitioner. What does this mean, and why does God do this?

3. Give some possible wrong motives when praying for revival.

4. What makes the striving and conflict of prayer a reality?

Perseverance in Prayer

Perseverance in Prayer (3)

Prevailing Prayer in the Bible

There are various examples illustrating this approach to prayer in the scriptures. Jacob's wrestling with the angel is a prime illustration (Gen. 32:1-32). God had already made covenant with him. He already had God's promises, yet he often tried to bring them to pass by his own scheming. After many years had passed by, and with the coming of Esau from whom he stole the birthright, his greatest scheme was devised. It was in this condition the angel of the Lord appeared to him in a wrestling match. In the end Jacob prevailed, but only after the socket of his hip was put out of joint! This touched Jacob's self-sufficiency. Later, he would worship, having to lean upon his staff (Heb. 11:21).

We wrestle with God in prayer. It seems as if God holds Himself back; He appears to seek to be part of us, until what is of the flesh, self, and spiritual slothfulness are drawn out of us and overcome. In so praying, the adversary is overcome, but God has prevailed over us. It is also true that we prevail with God so that He must bless us and make us princes. Jacob was showing a bold faith when he cried out to the angel, "I will not let you go unless you bless me!" (See Gen. 32:26.) It is this intensity that lies behind such verses as Mark 11:24 which states, "Therefore I say to you, whatever things you ask when you pray, believe that you receive them, and you will have them."

Abraham is another example. He called out to God six times on behalf of Sodom (Gen. 18:22-33). His nephew Lot was there. He prayed continuously, pressing more with God each time he took up the petition. He did not rest until he knew God had heard and promised. Through continuous prayer, he entered God's mind

Perseverance in Prayer

and found out God's will. Lot was saved from destruction because of Abraham (Gen. 19:29).

Elijah was a man of prayer. He prayed not once, but seven times
for rain (1 Kgs. 18: 41-46). He persevered, refusing to be de-
nied. He knew it would rain and yet he prayed seven times until
it came. The New Testament uses this story as an example of the
effective fervent pray of a righteous man that avails much
(James 5:16-18). This same passion was found in his successor,
Elisha, who after smiting the waters cries out, "Where is the
Lord God of Elijah?" (2 Kgs. 2:14).

Moses exercised importunity when interceding for the children
of Israel after they had sinned with the golden calf (Ex. 32 – 34).
The children of Israel had corrupted themselves and God said
He would destroy them and start over with Moses. It was the
intercession of Moses that held back the judgment. He wrestled
with God in prayer. His prayer was earnest, urging, well rea-
soned, importunate and unselfish. Israel was spared extinction
(Ex. 32:9-14). The people were forgiven though they would suffer discipline (Ex. 32:31-35).

God's decision concerning what he would do with the children
of Israel was not fully disclosed (Ex. 33:5). Moses continued to
petition God. Through prayer, he had the Lord commit Himself,
not just His angel, to be personally present with them (Ex. 33:2,
12-17). Moses continued to persuade God because he wanted to
see His glory and His goodness. The Lord passed by Moses and
proclaimed His name to His servant (Ex. 33: 18 – 34:7). Moses
pressed God further, until He renewed His covenant with Israel.
After warning them of the danger of idolatry, He gave them larger promises than before (Ex. 34:8-24). No wonder Moses' face
was shining when he came down from the mount!

Paul prayed three times before he received an answer to his cry. In so doing, he received the powerful influence of grace in his life by which he was able to minister in the most difficult situations (2 Cor. 12:7-10; 1 Cor. 15:10).

Undoubtedly, Jesus' prayer in the Garden of Gethsemane on the night of His betrayal is the most powerful example of importunate prayer described in Scripture (Lk. 22:39-46). He prayed three times there, because it appeared that the Father would not hear Him. He was heard on the basis of his godly fear for he submitted to the will of His Father (Heb. 5:7). His prayer was with strong crying and tears, so intense that His body sweat drops of blood. He prayed earnestly until He knew He was heard.

The first time He prayed in the Garden, He said, "O My Father, if it is possible, let this cup pass from Me; nevertheless, not as I will, but as You will." (See Matt. 26:39.) No answer was given from heaven.

The second time, His prayer was more direct with the words, "O My Father, if this cup cannot pass away from Me unless I drink it, Your will be done." (See Matt. 26:42.)

He prayed the third time with the same words, and heaven answered. His will was given up to God; his faith was proved and strengthened; and all temptation to yield to the flesh and the prince of this world was overcome. He rose from His knees as the High Priest. As a man, Jesus was tempted in all points, and yet without sin (Heb. 4:15). Though He was a Son, He learned obedience by the things He suffered (Heb. 5:8). He was dependent upon prayer.

The conflicts, strivings, and difficulties in prayer are the believer's highest privilege. To overcome yields the richest blessings. God would have us pray with importunity, persevere with intensity, refuse to accept denial, and spare nothing until the answer comes. As we pray with intensity, our whole being is given earnestly to God in fervent supplication. Boldness comes to lay hold of God's strength. Faith can be quiet and restful; it can be bold and passionate; it can be patient, and then swiftly lay claim to the promises of God. Faith knows that God hears prayer (Ps. 65:2); therefore, our prayer must be heard!

To continue praying for something requires a pure faith, because there may be no outward confirmation that anything is happening. The situation may even appear to be worse. Nevertheless, faith knows that God will answer prayer and will persevere.

In the parable of the widow, Jesus taught that we need to continually go to God in prayer, to cry unto Him day and night. We are not to faint, for God is not at all like the unjust judge. He yearns to grant the things for which we pray. He draws us out of ourselves in preparation for the requested blessing: He will avenge speedily. When the answer does come, it will come with great swiftness! Indeed, God hears and answers prayer!

The Privilege of Prayer

Thought Questions

1. Can you describe a season of prayer where you, like
    Abraham as he prayed for Sodom, pressed God further
    and further on an issue?

2. Describe the great gains Moses made as he continuously
    pressed the Lord when interceding for the children of Is-
    rael after they committed their sin with the golden calf?

3. Read 2 Corinthians 12:7-10. Paul declares that concern-
    ing the thorn in the flesh given to him, he pleaded with
    the Lord three times that it might depart from him. Is this
    a case of importunate praying? As a result of Paul's
    persistence, the Lord answered his prayer. What was
    God's response to Paul's prayers? What influence did
    this response have on Paul's attitude and future ministry?

4. Show the progression of prayer Jesus made as he ago-
    nized in the Garden of Gethsemane.

5. Why is a pure faith required when continuing to pray?

Perseverance in Prayer

Section Six

Pathway to Prayer

Section Six

Pathway to Prayer (1)

Conditions for Effective Prayer

God intends to provide answers to our prayers. It is He Who has given us the burden for prayer. The work of the ministry is initiated and sustained by importunate, persevering prayer. We are being trained for an eternal destiny as the Body of Christ, to rule and reign with Him in His inheritance throughout eternity. As we learn to pray with our whole being, we are changed and become better prepared to sit with Him on His throne. Meeting the conditions for effective prayer thus causes us to anticipate the glorious day of His return.

Jesus gave some of these conditions for answered prayer during His last evening with the disciples before He was tried and crucified. He spoke of many changes about to take place. In this context, He spoke of the prayer life that His followers should have:

Abiding in Christ – In John 15:1-16, Jesus spoke of bearing fruit. In verse 7, abiding in Christ, a condition for bearing fruit, is declared a prerequisite for answered prayer. Fruitfulness in our lives gives us power with God (John 15:16). This reinforces the concept that importunity is needed with God to prepare us to receive the answer He is willing to give. There is no doubt, according to Jesus, that the Father wishes our joy to be full and desires to answer our prayers.

To abide in Christ means to remain in fellowship with Him and to allow Christ to take possession of us. If we have been "grafted" into Christ, fruit bearing is the result of being properly related so that the life of the tree, the sap, may flow unhindered through the branch.

Abiding in Christ is a lifelong process in which the Spirit of God continues to take greater possession of our lives. To abide in Him, we must submit our minds and wills to Him and allow ourselves to become more like Christ, His mind and will becoming ours. As we grow in faith, obedience and love, our whole being will open up and receive a distinct and conscious union with Christ. Ultimately, He takes possession of our lives.

His Word Abiding in Us – As we are to abide in Christ, this same passage in Scripture (Jn. 15:1-16) tells us that Christ is to abide in us. He does that through His Word. As we allow His Word to abide in us, Christ dwells within. His word is to remain and be as comfortable in us as we would be in our own familiar homes.

Effectiveness in prayer is dependent upon hearing God's voice. We are to be acquainted with His teachings and incorporate them into our lives. The influence of His personal fellowship with us is absolutely vital. We need to apprehend by the Spirit what God is speaking to us. The living voice of God is to enter our hearts and produce positive disposition and conduct changes. Our outer life should be an exposition of the words of God within. As His words abide in us, His will rules us. Thus, we should constantly and diligently meditate upon His Word and be in fresh relationship, so that He may continue to speak.

In the Name of Jesus – The name of Jesus is the all-prevailing plea that moves the hand of God. Jesus, upon His ascension, is recognized as Lord of all. At His name, every knee should bow; every tongue should confess that He is Lord (Phil. 2:9-11). Jesus taught His disciples to use that name in prayer (Jn. 14:13-14; 15:16; 16:23-24,26).

What does it mean to use the name of another? To go in the name of another means that you have been given the power and authority to act as that person's representative or substitute. Without doubt, the person you represent must benefit from any transaction you make. You, vested with the general power of attorney, would soon be dismissed, if you used your position for personal gain.

The name of Jesus is not some sort of formula that guarantees an answer to prayer. It does not work like a magical charm. To pray in the name of the Lord means to have His interests at heart. Thus, to pray in Jesus' name is to ask the Father for something that will glorify the Son (Jn. 14:13-14). The Father's plan has always been for the sake of His Son; that is His ultimate goal in all He does. As we pray in Jesus' name, we must pray in such a way that Christ will receive glory when the Father responds to the prayer. The power we have with God in using the name of Jesus will depend on our degree of submission to those interests. Whatever we do, whether in word or deed, is to be done in the name of the Lord Jesus (Col. 3:17).

Ask what you desire – Jesus instructed us to ask what we desire (Jn. 15:7). He desires that our requests be definite. Often, our prayers are general and vague, while Jesus asks us to be specific.

Blind Bartimaeus heard that Jesus was passing by. He cried out in a general way for the Son of David to have mercy on him. When Jesus asked him to come near, He asked the blind man what he wanted. He had only asked for mercy. Was he asking for alms? Jesus wanted Bartimaeus to be specific (Mk. 10:46-52). To a man who had been infirm for thirty-eight years, who

Pathway to Prayer

had hoped that someone would assist him into the pool when the angle stirred up the water, Jesus asked, "Do you want to be made well?" (See Jn. 5:6.)

How much prayer is vague? How much prayer is not specific or pointed? Do we know our own needs? Do we honestly and definitely know the will of God? Are our desires honest and real? Are we ready to persevere? Do we have personal and pointed dealings with God? Do we just have a multitude of requests or do we see that each individual request is thought out and we expect it to be answered?

Jesus does not ask, "What do you want?" The question is rather, "What do you will?" We can want certain things; perhaps, we don't really will them. A person may want to be rich, but if he doesn't put his will into it he never will be rich! The will rules the heart and life. Is what we pray for just a wish, or is it the mind of God? Are we content with unanswered prayer? Do we purpose to have what we ask? Let us be definite in our requests to God, and fully expect the Lord to specifically fulfill all our petitions (Ps. 20:5).

The Privilege of Prayer

Thought Questions

1. "Fruit bearing is the result of being properly related so that the life of the tree, the sap, may flow unhindered through the branch." Discuss the analogy the author uses here. To what or whom do the following refer: fruit, tree, branch, sap?

2. Explain how it is possible for Christ to abide in you.

3. Complete this statement: To pray in the name of Jesus means _____.

4. "The answer to prayer should cause the Father to be glorified (praised, honored, worshipped) in the Son." Suggest a prayer that you have said or heard that caused the Father to be glorified in His Son.

Pathway to Prayer (2)

Hindrances to Effective Prayer

Every believer must have an intimate prayer life and be able to receive from God daily what is needed. The eyes of the Lord are on the righteous and His ears are open to their prayers (1 Pet. 3:12). Rightness is a condition for answered prayers. This means a practical righteousness that is visibly demonstrated. Righteousness, like fruit bearing, holds power with God. The effective, fervent prayer of a righteous man avails much (James 5:16). A righteous life that earnestly prays will be effective in its working. **Lack of righteousness is a hindrance to effective prayer.** The following hindrances all stem from a lack of righteousness.

Improper Relationships – Peter assumes that husbands and wives pray together (1 Pet. 3:7). One's spouse is the obvious and logical person with whom one should pray (c.f. 1 Cor. 7:3-5). Peter thus exhorts husbands to dwell properly with their wives, so that their prayers are not hindered. In many situations, it is observable that many believers look for a "prayer partner" in someone else besides their spouse. This is wrong. If a marriage is honoring to God, and the will of God is sought, why shouldn't husbands and wives seek God together?

Husbands and wives must treat each other with respect and courtesy, fulfilling each other's needs. Obviously, stress in the day-to-day relationships is not conducive to a couple pouring out their hearts to God together! Husbands and wives are one unit before God, and as Christians they have the same hope, desires and service. They should fast and pray together, teach and support each other, share one another's trials, conceal nothing from each other and together praise God. It is the prayer together that brings the blessedness of the Holy Spirit into the relationship. If a husband and wife can't break through their timidity to pray together, it is doubtful if they can share much else in life on any deep and meaningful level. Those that pray together won't easily sin against each other.

Wrong Motives – James declares that we ask and have not because we ask amiss, that we may spend it on our own pleasures (James 4:2-3). Many times we can be self-centered instead of God-centered. Are we concerned with our own ease and comfort, or are we concerned for God's name, honor, glory and kingdom? Prayer is the working out of God's will, not our whims.

The answer to prayer should cause the Father to be glorified in the Son (Jn. 14:13). Whatever we do should be for the glory of God (1 Cor. 10:31). Where Jesus is Lord, God the Father is glorified (Phil. 2:11). This is the aim of prayer.

Sin – Sin takes away confidence, stripping us of boldness as we go before God with our requests. There are numerous scriptures that speak this truth. A heart free from condemnation is a prerequisite (1 Jn. 3:21-22).

Sin is a barrier to answered prayer. The Lord's hand is not shortened that He cannot save; nor His ear heavy, that He cannot hear, but sin separates us from God who answers prayer (Is. 59:1-2). The psalmist knew that iniquity regarded in the heart causes the Lord not to hear (Ps. 66:18). The prayer of a person who turns his ear from hearing the law is an abomination to the Lord (Pro. 28:9). Prayer cannot pass through to God because of sin (Lam. 3:8,44). When the children of Israel shut their ears to the law and the prophets, God shut His ear to them (Zech. 7:8-13).

The Privilege of Prayer

It is no wonder, then, that the psalmist asked God to unite his heart in the fear of the Lord (Ps. 86:11), to search him, and to see if there be any wicked way in him. The psalmist yearned to walk in the way everlasting (Ps. 139:23-24).

Idols in the heart – God refused to hear the prayers of hypocritical believers, who outwardly sought God, but inwardly had idols in their hearts (Eze. 14:3). The heart must be clean (Ps. 51:10). We are to love God not just outwardly, but with all our hearts. This is the first commandment (Matt. 22:37-38).

Lack of Compassion – The will of the Father is to do works of love. The love of God that is poured out in our hearts by the Holy Spirit (Rom. 5:5) is to reach out to humanity. If we shut our ears to the cries of the poor, we will not be heard when we cry out in need (Pro. 21:13). How can we have confidence toward God when our hearts are cold toward others in need (1 Jn. 3:16-24)? Fasting and almsgiving are represented in Scripture as the wings of prayer (Matt. 6:1-18; Acts 10:2,30; Is. 58:6-7).

Doubt – To doubt means to entertain a second opinion. If we waiver on what God has spoken, we will never persevere to the end to receive (James 1:6-8). Peter sank in the water because he took note of the wind and the waves. Fear caused him to doubt, in spite of the Lord's command to come to him (Matt. 14:28-31).

Unforgiveness – Scripture makes more than one reference to this hindrance to answered prayer. Faith in God to move mountains simply cannot flood the heart that is filled with unforgiveness (Mk. 11:22-26). Faith works through love (Gal. 5:6). When we chose not to forgive and hold bitterness and grudges (whether we are wronged or just think we are), we are sacrificing power in prayer. We are to forgive others if we want to be forgiven (Matt. 6:12,14-15). We will be held accountable and disciplined by the Lord if we do not forgive others (Matt. 18:35).

Lack of Gratitude – We are invited to bring the whole of our lives to God. We are to be anxious for nothing, but commit all things to God in prayer with thanksgiving (Phil. 4:6-7). Praise should be on our lips when we go to God. We are to be vigilant in prayer with thanksgiving (Col. 4:2). Christian life is to be rooted in thanksgiving (Col. 2:7).

All we do is to be done in the name of the Lord, giving thanks to God by Him (Col. 3:17). We need an attitude of gratitude as exemplified by the one leper who returned to give thanks (Lk. 17:11-19). We should be definite in thanking God for past blessings as we seek him for new ones. Most of the apostle Paul's epistles begin with thanksgiving in prayer. Notice that the command to pray without ceasing is sandwiched between the commands to rejoice always and to give thanks in everything (1 Thess. 5:16-18).

The Privilege of Prayer

Thought Questions

1. Why do improper relationships create a hindrance to answered prayer?

2. What is the ultimate true motive in prayer that should master all other motives?

3. Suggest some idols that believers may have in their hearts, causing answers to prayer to be delayed.

4. Why do you think Jesus made frequent reference to unforgiveness as a major obstacle to answered prayer?

5. Describe the importance of gratitude as a condition for answered prayer. Why is it a condition?

6. James 4:3 declares, "You ask and do not receive, because you ask amiss," Suggest something you have asked God for that you have not received from Him. Which one(s) of the hindrances to prayer stated in this section might be responsible for this situation?

Pathway to Prayer (3)

Prayer and Holiness

Holiness is the nature of God. Therefore, without holiness, no man will see the Lord (Heb. 12:14). To be effective in prayer, fruit bearing and personal righteousness are essential. Intercession is the gift of the Holy Spirit, and He is grieved in the presence of sin. This makes intercession a reality in the heart of the believer, as the Holy Spirit yearns for deliverance from the very presence of sin in this fallen world (Rom. 8:14-30).

Because of this, great intercessors feel the pain of sin. They cry out to God in confession of sin, for their own and for that of others. Daniel, described throughout Scripture as having remarkably positive character, sought God with prayer, supplications, fasting, sackcloth and ashes. He made his confession, recounting the sins of his people (Dan. 9:1-21, especially 4 & 20). Nehemiah, who built the walls of Jerusalem, had the same experience. He felt very keenly the sin of his people before God and poured out his soul in confession (Neh. 1:4-11, especially 6 & 7).

All great confessions of faith are coupled with a deep sense of humility. The Canaanite woman whose daughter was freed from a tormenting demon took a lowly position before Jesus. Yet, the Lord reckoned her as one having great faith (Matt. 15:21-28). The Roman centurion did not consider himself worthy to have the Lord enter under his roof, but he likewise was commended as an example of great faith (Lk. 7:1-10). When an enemy too large for Jehoshaphat surrounded him, he confessed his own lack of might or the knowledge of what to do, and he looked to the Lord (2 Chron. 20:12).

Pathway to Prayer

If we desire to be intercessors, we likewise must be clothed with humility. We are vessels through whom the Holy Spirit makes intercession. The power to minister is of God, not of ourselves (2 Cor. 4:7). Sensitivity to the Holy Spirit is a must. Grieving the Holy Spirit must not take place (Eph. 4:30). The closer we draw nigh to God, the greater the sense of personal shortcomings is recognized in our lives. In the presence of the Lord, Isaiah described himself and the people around him as having "unclean lips." (See Is. 6:1,5) One of Peter's initial responses to Christ included a sense of his own sinfulness (Lk. 5:8).

As we draw nigh to God, we become increasingly aware that Christ is our righteousness, and that the flesh profits nothing. We are not yet glorified and sin is still a present reality. If the Holy Spirit is to fill our lives so that we can walk in His strength and power, we must hunger and thirst for righteousness and purity of heart (Matt. 5:6,8). This is not to be confused with Satan's accusations that are aimed at crippling us, but we are to remember from whence we have come and marvel at God's redeeming grace (2 Pet. 1:9).

Paul, the apostle, was a great man of prayer. Yet, he carried a tremendous sense of humility as well. Reflecting upon his earlier lifestyle and the great load of sin for which he had been forgiven, he considered himself less than the least of all saints. Indeed, Paul attributed his ability to minister to God's sufficient grace (Eph. 3:8). He ascribed his abundant labors not to himself but to the grace of God that was with him (1 Cor. 15:9-10). Paul cited himself as an example of the grace of God in saving a person's life (1 Tim. 1:12-16). None of us merits the grace of God or is worthy of His calling. It is His grace alone that gets the glory. Paul understood this well (Gal. 1:15-16).

The Privilege of Prayer

This sense needs to be developed in those who will give themselves over to intercession. Sin is still a present reality; only at the resurrection will this change. Our joy is that we are monuments of God's redeeming grace. We thank God for the gift of the Holy Spirit whereby we are enabled by His grace to live victorious lives before Him, in spite of the fact that sin is still abundantly evident in this world.

As we draw close to God in prayer, He progressively reveals His holiness and demands that we become holy, as He is holy. The revelation of His holiness brought a much greater level of humility into the lives of Abraham, Jacob, Job, Isaiah and others. It will bring us low in our own eyes as well and exalt the Christ who died for us, intercedes for us, and lives within us to become all things to us.

This produces a continuous yearning after the righteousness of Christ to be formed within us until that perfect day. Jesus Christ is made unto us wisdom, righteousness, sanctification, and redemption (1 Cor. 1:30). True intercession sees righteousness as its life, for it is righteousness worked into the life of the believer that gives him prevailing power with God.

Peter indicates that a believer can forget from whence he came (2 Pet. 1:9). If we do not press on to know the Lord, we can easily lose our sensitivity toward sin. Our conscience can be immunized against it. No longer horrified with disobedience or appalled at worldliness, we feel no conviction for being cold toward spiritual things or for our lack of fervency. We lose the power to mourn over sin.

Not only can we lose the power to mourn over sin, but also we can easily entertain it. We become accustomed to sin; it draws no cry of remorse from us, because we are blind to the fact that we have drifted. God yielded up His Son to the horrors of Calvary so that sin might not reign, and yet, we become passive toward it.

Failure in prayer is the reason for failure in the Christian life. We are to keep in constant fellowship with God and watch and pray lest we fall into temptation (Matt. 26:41). Not to consider communion with God a priority in our lives is a reproach to Him, a mockery of His grace. By the shed blood of Jesus, we are invited into the throne room in the courts of heaven and we spurn the invitation because we are too busy. Our growth into the likeness of Christ is in exact proportion to the time and heart we put into prayer. A prayer life brings the blessing. The closer we draw to God the greater the desire for our hearts to be clean and the greater the need for it.

We are to pray, "Do not lead us not into temptation." (See Matt. 6:13) The psalmist cries out to be cleansed from secret faults and presumptuous sins and that the words of his mouth and the meditation of his heart would be acceptable in the Lord's sight (Ps. 19:12-14). It is with clean hands and a pure heart that we can ascend into the hill of the Lord and stand in His holy place (Ps. 24:3-5). God answers the prayer of a righteous man because he fears Him. Absolute and unlimited devotion to Christ's service has power in the courts of heaven.

Because Abraham was a powerful intercessor, Lot was delivered from the fate of Sodom. Nevertheless, Abraham lived a life of total obedience, even if it meant the sacrifice of his own son. Thus, as a friend, God revealed to Abraham His intentions (Gen. 18:17-22).

Who cannot marvel at the gains Moses made in prayer? Yet, Moses was the humblest man on the face of the earth (Num.

12:3), and faithful in the Lord's house (Num. 12:7). He chose suffering affliction with the people of God rather than possessing the treasures of Egypt (Heb. 11:24-27).

It is righteousness that gives you power to pray. Righteousness is appalled at sin and extols the holiness of God. Elijah, a man of prayer, challenged the people of his day: "How long will you falter between two opinions? If the Lord is God, follow Him." (See 1 Kgs. 18:21.)

Let us be encouraged that God desires to answer prayer. Take up the privilege of prayer, of working together with Him in fulfilling the eternal purpose for His Son. Let us be encouraged to lift our voices before God.

> Therefore the Lord will wait, that He may be gracious to you; And therefore He will be exalted, that He may have mercy on you. For the Lord is a God of justice; Blessed are all those who wait for Him. For the people shall dwell in Zion at Jerusalem; You shall weep no more. He will be very gracious to you at the sound of your cry; When He hears it, He will answer you. (Is. 30:18-19)

> But know that the Lord has set apart for Himself him who is godly; the Lord will hear when I call to Him. (Ps. 4:3)

> I have called upon You, for you will hear me, O God; Incline Your ear to me, and hear my speech. (Ps. 17:6)

> O You who hear prayer, To You all flesh will come. (Ps. 65:2)

Therefore I will look to the Lord; I will wait for the God of my salvation; My God will hear me. (Micah 7:7)

Now this is the confidence that we have in Him, that if we ask anything according to His will, He hears us. And if we know that He hears us, whatever we ask, we know that we have the petitions that we have asked of Him (1 Jn. 5:14-15).

The Privilege of Prayer

Thought Questions

1. Explain the concept that great intercessors feel the pain of sin. Can you give biblical examples, as well as examples from modern church history? Do you personally sense the Holy Spirit's grief at the presence of sin?

2. How is it that great confessions of faith are coupled with a deep sense of humility?

3. Absolute and unlimited devotion to Christ has power in the courts of heaven. Expound on this comment.

4. Why does righteousness give us power in prayer?

Pathway to Prayer

Section Seven

Participating in Christ's Prayer

135

Section Seven

Participating in Christ's Prayer

Lifted into the Communion of the Godhead

We have studied some important concepts:

The Holy Spirit is our provision.

The work of God depends on prayer.

God does not desire to act until we pray.

The conditions for answered prayer must be met.

Perseverance in prayer until the answer comes is essential.

Prayer prepares us for participation in God's eternal purpose for His Son.

At the cross, Jesus made intercession for the transgressors (Is. 53:12). Now, seated at the right hand of Majesty on High, He continues as our faithful High Priest to make intercession for us (Rom. 8:34; Heb. 7:25).

The Christian life is one of participation in Christ. Through union with His death we are free from the guilt of sin and its power. We are delivered from the old man. Through union with His resurrection, we are brought to a new life and have become a new creation. We have been given a reigning life of victory and power, by union with His ascension. The Christian life is more than receiving the benefits of the work of Christ on our

Participating in Christ's Prayer

behalf; indeed, it requires a participation in those events. The same is true of the work of intercession.

Is intercession the saying of "our" prayers to God? Are worship and praise "our" gifts to God? A much more accurate view would be to see the love relationship between the Father and the Son. The Father loves the Son, and the Son loves the Father. Jesus came from the Father into the world to do His Father's will. John's gospel is abundantly clear on this matter. When Jesus had accomplished all His Father gave Him to do, He returned back to the Father (Jn. 13:1; 17:4-5). Jesus has both a mission from the Father to the world and a role as our High Priest before the Father.

From this view of the believer's participation in Christ, worship is sharing with Christ in His adoration of the Father. Prayer is joining with Christ in His intercession to the Father. Evangelism is Christ's mission from the Father to the world. By being baptized into Christ, we are lifted into the very life of the Godhead! This is in accordance with the prayer of Jesus in Jn. 17:21, just before He was crucified: "that they all may be as one, as You, Father, are in Me, and I in You; that they may be one in Us; that the world may believe that You have sent Me."

The gift of the Holy Spirit is to make actual our participation in Christ. The Holy Spirit reproduces in us what Jesus speaks in intercession to the Father (Rom. 8:26-27,34). The burden we feel is that which fills the heart of Christ as He remembers each of us to the Father, as He obtains from Him the resources required for the fulfillment of His will.

To pray in the Spirit is to participate in the very eternal fellowship and communion of the Persons of the Godhead! This is a privilege beyond comprehension! Who will give themselves over to such an honor? Let us not be slack in pursuit of such a privilege. The gift of the Spirit makes all of this possible. It is not "our" prayer, but the Spirit of the Son that cries within our hearts (Gal. 4:6). Intercession is the ministry of the Holy Spirit.

As we join together, even now, with the Godhead, we are being prepared for our eternal destiny as the Body of Christ, as joint-heirs together with Him. We shall enter into glory with Him! Prayer is the means of preparation for such a call as this. Let us, without hesitation, pursue the golden privilege of prayer!

Participating in Christ's Prayer

Thought Questions

1. What is the difference between us saying 'our' prayers, and the Spirit of God reproducing the prayers of the Son of God in our hearts? What implications does this have for being Spirit-led in prayer?

2. Explore more fully the concept that the Holy Spirit causes us to be a participant in Christ. Include discussions on prayer, worship and missions.

3. Prayer is the means of preparation for our eternal destiny as the Body of Christ. How does such a truth motivate the church to Spirit-filled, persevering believing prayer?

For Further Reading

Brandt, R. L., (1981), Tongues, the Greatest Gift, Bridge
Publishing, South Plainfield, New Jersey

Cornwall, Judson, (1999), Ascending to Glory, Kingdom
Publishing, Mansfield, PA

Cornwall, Judson (1990), Praying the Scriptures, Creation
House, Lake Mary, Florida

Fromke, DeVern, (1986) Life's Ultimate Privilege, Sure
Foundation, Cloverdale, In.

Fromke, DeVern, (1982) The Ultimate Intention, Sure
Foundation, Cloverdale, In.

Murray, Andrew, (1961), Let Us Draw Nigh, Christian
Literature Crusade, Fort Washington, PA

Murray, Andrew, (1982), The Believer's School of Prayer,
Bethany House Publishers, Minneapolis, Minnesota

Murray, Andrew, (1981), the Ministry of Intercession, Christian
Literature Crusade, Bristol, United Kingdom

Murray, Andrew (1980), The Secret of Believing Prayer,
Bethany Fellowship, Minneapolis, Minnesota

Nee, Watchman, (1977), Let Us Pray, Christian Fellowship
Publishers, Inc., New York

Nee, Watchman, (1973), The Prayer Ministry of the Church, Christian Fellowship Publishers, Inc., New York

Torrey, R. A. (1982) How to Pray, Moody Press, Chicago, Ill.

Torrey, R. A. (1971) The Power of Prayer, Zondervan Publishing, Grand Rapids, Michigan

Wallis, Arthur, (1970) Pray in the Spirit, Kingsway Publications, Eastbourne, England

Word & Worship Global Outreach
Eugene & Darla Smith

**A ministry of
Teaching, Music and Missions**

**For more information about WWGO,
visit their website:**

www.wwgo.ca

Printed in the United States
27854LVS00001B/115-378

9 781931 178594